WENSLEYDALE

Paul Hannon

HILLSIDE

HILLSIDE GUIDES - ACROSS THE NORTH & BEYOND

The Uplands of Britain
•**THE HIGH PEAKS OF ENGLAND & WALES**
•**YORKSHIRE DALES, MOORS & FELLS**

Long Distance Walks
•COAST TO COAST WALK   •DALES WAY   •CLEVELAND WAY
•CUMBRIA WAY   •WESTMORLAND WAY   •FURNESS WAY
•BRONTE WAY   •PENDLE WAY   •NIDDERDALE WAY
•LADY ANNE'S WAY   •TRANS-PENNINE WAY   •CALDERDALE WAY

Hillwalking - Lake District
•LAKELAND FELLS - SOUTH   •LAKELAND FELLS - EAST
•LAKELAND FELLS - NORTH   •LAKELAND FELLS - WEST

Circular Walks - Peak District
•NORTHERN PEAK   •EASTERN PEAK   •CENTRAL PEAK
•SOUTHERN PEAK   •WESTERN PEAK

Circular Walks - Yorkshire Dales
•HOWGILL FELLS   •THREE PEAKS   •MALHAMDALE
•WHARFEDALE   •NIDDERDALE   •WENSLEYDALE   •SWALEDALE

Circular Walks - North York Moors
•WESTERN MOORS   •SOUTHERN MOORS

Circular Walks - South Pennines
•BRONTE COUNTRY   •ILKLEY MOOR
•CALDERDALE   •SOUTHERN PENNINES

Circular Walks - Lancashire
•BOWLAND   •PENDLE & THE RIBBLE   •WEST PENNINE MOORS

Circular Walks - North Pennines
•TEESDALE   •EDEN VALLEY   •ALSTON & ALLENDALE

WayMaster Guides - Short Scenic Walks
•ESKDALE, North York Moors   •WHARFEDALE, Yorkshire Dales
•AMBLESIDE & LANGDALE, Lake District

City Theme Walks   •YORK WALKS

Pocket Biking Guides
•WHARFEDALE BIKING GUIDE
•AIRE VALLEY BIKING GUIDE   •CALDERDALE BIKING GUIDE

WayMaster Visitor Guides •YORKSHIRE DALES

Send for a detailed current catalogue and pricelist,
and also visit *www.hillsidepublications.co.uk*

WALKING COUNTRY

WENSLEYDALE

Paul Hannon

HILLSIDE

HILLSIDE
PUBLICATIONS
12 Broadlands
Keighley
West Yorkshire
BD20 6HX

First published in 1987
Updated and extended 1996
9th impression 2004

ISBN 1 870141 43 1

Cover illustration:
Aysgarth Falls
Back cover: Middleham Castle; Semerwater; West Burton
(Paul Hannon/Hillslides Picture Library)

Page 1: Countersett Old Hall
Page 3: Horsehouse

Printed in Great Britain by
Carnmor Print
95-97 London Road
Preston
Lancashire
PR1 4BA

CONTENTS

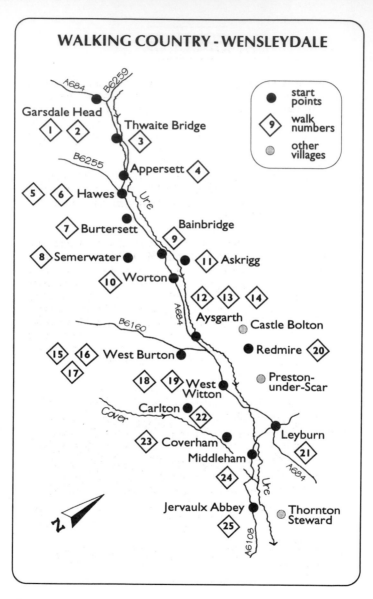

WALKING COUNTRY - WENSLEYDALE

start points

9 walk numbers

other villages

Garsdale Head
1 2
Thwaite Bridge
3
Appersett 4
Hawes
5 6
Burtersett
7 Bainbridge
9
Semerwater
8 Askrigg 11
Worton
10
12 13 14
Aysgarth
Castle Bolton
Redmire 20
West Burton
15 16
17 Preston-under-Scar
West Witton
18 19
Carlton
22
Coverham 23
Leyburn
Middleham 21
24
Jervaulx Abbey
25 Thornton Steward

N

INTRODUCTION

Wensleydale is a broad green valley with innumerable hidden features that more than make amends for its lack of instant grandeur. Here one must make an effort to seek out the attractions, and the ensuing pages lead the discerning walker to a host of splendid sights. An oft-made claim that this is Yorkshire's major dale is a point that Wharfedale would surely debate, unless the many side-valleys and the fertile pastures downstream of the National Park boundary are included. These lesser valleys are something unique to Wensleydale, for Coverdale, Walden, Bishopdale, Raydale and several more are all sizeable dales in their own right. Each contributes its share to the Wensleydale scene.

The individuality of the valley is also exhibited by its very name. This is the only major dale not to take its title from the river. The Ure - anciently the Yore, a name still applied in some quarters - lost out to the village of Wensley which lies just outside the Park on the road to Leyburn. This the Dales' most fertile valley was once a great hunting forest, and other associations with history involve a Brigantes' hill-fort, Iron age lake dwellings, a Roman road, a Roman fort, a 13th century abbey, a 14th century castle, a 15th century fortified manor house, a 16th century beacon site, a 17th century hall, and traces of lead and coal-mining and of quarrying. Not bad for starters!

Upper Falls, Aysgarth

The natural attractions surely deserve a mention now. It will be noticed that not many walks take in the riverbank, for a good deal of its course is without rights of way: the river itself leads an uneventful life other than one or two famous moments which all who have visited the dale will already know, and if not, will soon be acquainted with. Neither are the high tops very inviting to gentler walkers, indeed the bulk of Wensleydale's walking is to be had somewhere between the two extremities. The physical structure of the dale gives us a series of regular ledges on which some superb walking can be found. These mid-height terraces also generally provide the best views.

Having mentioned the National Park boundary, it should be borne in mind that there are equally fine attractions outwith this arbitrary line, and so downstream we find some fine walking around Middleham, Leyburn and Jervaulx. The crowning glory of Wensleydale however, despite the Ure's general lack of interest, are the waterfalls. Nowhere else can boast such a fine array of tumbling falls, for most of the side valleys also proudly possess their own force. These are the gems that make Wensleydale special.

THE COUNTRY CODE
- Respect the life and work of the countryside
- Protect wildlife, plants and trees
- Keep to public paths across farmland
- Safeguard water supplies
- Go carefully on country roads
- Keep dogs under control
- Guard against all risks of fire
- Fasten all gates
- Leave no litter - take it with you
- Make no unnecessary noise
- Leave livestock, crops and machinery alone
- Use gates and stiles to cross fences, hedges and walls

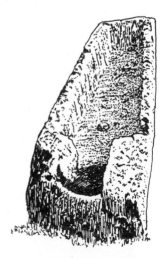

Stone coffin at the Templars' Chapel, under Penhill

Getting around

Hawes and Aysgarth are perhaps the best known centres in the dale, though the area is normally approached from Leyburn, which has the best bus links with points further afield. The main bus service runs along the dale floor to Hawes, using different routes that between them serve most of the villages. With a little planning, any number of permutations can be created by linking different sections of the walks, to create longer routes or to take advantage of public transport. Many of the starting points are served by bus.

Using the guide

Each walk is self-contained, with essential information being followed by a simple map and concise description of the route. Dovetailed between this are useful notes of features along the way, and interspersed are illustrations which both capture the flavour of the walks and record the many items of interest. In order to make the instructions easier to follow, essential route description has been highlighted in bold type, while items in lighter type refer to historical asides and things to look out for: in this format you can find your way more easily while still locating features of interest at the relevant point in the text. Please remember to obey legitimate signs encountered on your walks: rights of way can be opened, closed or diverted. On these occasions the official notices should take precedence over the guidebook.

The simple sketch maps identify the location of the routes rather than the fine detail, and whilst the route description should be sufficient to guide you around, an Ordnance Survey map is recommended. The route as depicted can easily be plotted on the relevant OS map. To gain the most from a walk, the remarkable detail of the 1:25,000 scale maps cannot be matched: they also serve to vary walks as desired, giving an improved picture of one's surroundings and the availability of linking paths. This area is fortunate in that one sheet gives coverage of most of the walks. The relevant maps for each walk are as follows:-

- **Outdoor Leisure 19** - Howgill Fells/Upper Eden Valley: 1-4
- **Outdoor Leisure 30** - Yorkshire Dales North/Central: 5-24
- **Explorer 302** - Northallerton & Thirsk: 24-25

Also extremely useful for general planning purposes are the Landranger sheets, at 1:50,000. The following pair cover the area:

98 - Wensleydale & Upper Wharfedale
99 - Northallerton & Ripon

HELL GILL

START *Garsdale Head*   *Grid ref. SD 797926*

DISTANCE *7¼ miles*

ORDNANCE SURVEY MAPS
1:50,000
Landranger 98 - Wensleydale & Upper Wharfedale
1:25,000
Outdoor Leisure 19 - Howgill Fells/Upper Eden Valley

ACCESS *Start from the Moorcock Inn at the junction of the Kirkby Stephen road with the Hawes-Sedbergh road. There is ample roadside parking. Garsdale station on the Settle-Carlisle line is a mile away.*

A bracing walk through grand upland environs.

S The strategic position of the *Moorcock* places it in that small band of well known (from the outside at least) outpost-hostelries. **From the pub head down the Kirkby Stephen road and leave it at a farm drive on the right bound for Yore House. After crossing the Ure (choice of bridges) turn left on a sketchy track upstream. Though it falters somewhat, continue on to meet the drive to Blades as it bridges the river, and follow it to the right.**

Blades is the only farm we encounter which is still operating. The prominent white building on the hillside above-left is the former youth hostel at Shaws, visited in the adjacent WALK 3. **At Blades pass between the buildings and at the end take a gate on the right. A track crosses the field to another gate, and a detour through two more gives access to the steep pasture behind. When the sketchy way bears left to a gate at the top follow it, maintaining this uphill course**

to the derelict farm of High Dike. Use gates to its right to get onto the open fell. High Dike was once an inn catering for travellers on the old road.

Running alongside the intake wall is a track: this is the High Way and it runs left on a generally level course all the way to Hell Gill Bridge. It is best known as part of the route taken by Lady Anne Clifford when visiting her Westmorland castles in the 17th century. Now a route for more leisurely travellers, it had for centuries before formed the major 'highway' through the valley to Kirkby Stephen until the arrival of the turnpike road - the present road turning off at the *Moorcock* - in 1825. Though the High Way is steeped in history, its one perpetual feature is the improving prospect of majestic Wild Boar Fell across the valley.

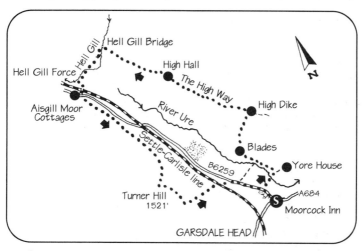

For the most part the wall stays with us, and when it eventually parts company the track runs on to the top of a line of trees above a gorge. This last beck before Hell Gill Bridge is in fact the infant Ure, within 1½ miles of its birthplace on Lunds Fell. The rugged little gorge is one of its few lively moments outside of Aysgarth. **The way continues on by small outcrops to quickly reach Hell Gill Bridge.** This stone-built structure straddles Hell Gill Beck as it transforms into the Eden, and beneath is a limestone gorge up to 60ft deep. The Yorkshire-Westmorland border (and modern equivalent) follows the beck down to the road, so from the bridge to the cottages we make our only foray out of Yorkshire. The National Park shares this boundary.

11

On crossing the bridge turn immediately left through a gate to descend a track to the cottage of Hell Gill and then out down the drive. With a railway bridge just ahead be sure to deviate right a few yards for a dramatic appraisal of Hell Gill Force. This splendid waterfall makes a vertical drop over a cliff, particularly impressive in view of the infancy of the stream. Be warned that youngsters should be on a tight rein here.

Crossing the railway bridge the road is joined at Aisgill Moor Cottages. Though they overlook the Settle-Carlisle line and the county boundary, they in turn are most emphatically overlooked by Wild Boar Fell, one of the Pennines' finest mountains. There is also a welcome opportunity for refreshment at Aisgill Crafts. Just south of the cottages is Aisgill Summit, at 1169 feet the highest point on a main line in Britain.

Aisgill Moor Cottages and Wild Boar Fell

Cross the road to a gate onto the moor and then follow the fence left to a wall. Though initially pathless the way is straightforward, with a wall, for the most part, for company. An occasionally sketchy way runs on to the barns of High Shaw Paddock, shortly after which a large tract of rough pasture is entered. An intermittent path slants across to the head of a small beck before rising up above a marshy section to a gate in the fence.

Here we gain the long - and by this stage broad - ridge descending from Swarth Fell, and follow it left over the minor dome of Turner Hill. This is an excellent viewpoint, chiefly for the fine surround of fells. Besides a good stretch of railway, the best single feature is the entire length of Wensleydale stretching into the haze. Continue down the wall-side to a stile by a gate, and from it vacate the ridge by descending the rather rough pasture on the left to a highly prominent footbridge high above the railway. A track heads away to join the road, with the *Moorcock* only a few minutes along to the right.

Hell Gill Force,
(Mallerstang Edge behind)

13

2

GRISEDALE

START *Garsdale Head*   *Grid ref. SD 787917*

DISTANCE *3¾ miles*

ORDNANCE SURVEY MAPS
1:50,000
Landranger 98 - Wensleydale & Upper Wharfedale
1:25,000
Outdoor Leisure 19 - Howgill Fells/Upper Eden Valley

ACCESS *Start from the station on the Settle-Carlisle line. There is parking on the road climbing from the main road to the station.*

An unglamorous stroll through a bleak Dales upland - great!

S Garsdale Station is an isolated spot, known as Hawes Junction when the Wensleydale branch from Northallerton existed. It is ideally placed for hopping off for a day on the lonely fells where the valleys of Garsdale, Wensleydale and Mallerstang all form. Here the rivers Clough, Ure and Eden (respectively) set their courses for very different points of the compass. The Clough merges into the Rawthey and in turn the Lune to reach the sea at Morecambe Bay; the Ure eventually joins the Ouse and flows into the North Sea via the Humber; while the Eden remains its own boss all the way to the Solway Firth.

Descend to the main road and cross straight over to a stile. Head straight up the pasture to the next stile, from where the waterfall of Clough Force can be espied by a detour to the left. Prominent across Grisedale are the stone men on Grisedale Pike, a shoulder of the immense mountain, Baugh Fell. **Back on top, maintain a direct line for Grisedale across a couple of rough pastures of Garsdale Low Moor with wall-stiles in between. A prominent tree guides us towards the farm buildings of Blake Mire. From a stile to the right,**

a series of stiles slant down to the valley. **Without immediately joining the road, take a stile by some barns to remain parallel with it, only meeting it at Moor Rigg beyond a further stile.**

Grisedale is a hidden valley brought to public attention by a 1970s TV documentary highlighting the disastrous demise of its farms. **Turn right along the now unenclosed road as far as its terminus at East House, then continue up the track onto the open moor. Fork right by the intake wall, and as the way fades curve steadily left on a level course to see both stile and gate in the wall ahead.** Up to the left is Turner Hill, a brief levelling of the ridge descending from Swarth Fell.

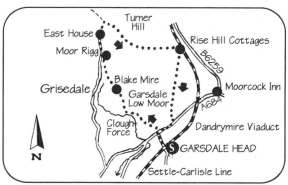

Beyond the wall descend rough pasture to a footbridge over the railway at Rise Hill Cottages. Do not cross it, but squeeze between the line and the house and head diagonally away to a collapsed wall. Rising behind, use a depression between two gentle slopes to locate a stile. From here there is a good view of Dandymire Viaduct, and to its right Garsdale station. **Now a sketchy trod picks a way across two further pastures before a direct descent to the main road, emerging opposite a farm. The road junction is now two minutes to the right.**

Swarth Fell from Blake Mire

3

THE HIGH WAY

START *Thwaite Bridge*   *Grid ref. SD 826922*

DISTANCE *6½ miles*

ORDNANCE SURVEY MAPS
1:50,000
Landranger 98 - Wensleydale & Upper Wharfedale
1:25,000
Outdoor Leisure 19 - Howgill Fells/Upper Eden Valley

ACCESS *Start from the large lay-by alongside the bridge. It is located on the A684 midway between Appersett and the Moorcock Inn.*

An easy walk, mixed pastures on the outward leg contrasting with an ancient highway along the fellside above for the return.

S Thwaite Bridge is illustrated on page 21. **Cross the bridge to the farm at Thwaite Bridge House and turn into the yard. At once take a gate on the right and head away to a stile in the wall corner beyond. Advance to another stile then away with the wall, taking a stile over it part-way on. Resume along the foot of a large pasture, a thin path running on above some trees to a stile in the far corner. A thin trod runs on through rough pasture to the base of Cotterside Plantation.**

Down below the playful Ure winds away: across it are the vast slopes of Widdale Fell, while ahead Baugh Fell forms the skyline. A small viaduct on the Settle-Carlisle line north of the *Moorcock Inn* is visible, and the more substantial Dandrymire Viaduct soon appears further to the left. **From the stile there advance on again, meeting a track just short of the gate at the end. This slants down as a fine green way and runs on to Yore House. Behind the farm is a ladder-stile beneath a wood.** In 1996 the guidepost here still pointed the way to Garsdale Head Youth Hostel, which last welcomed hostellers in the early 1980s! Around this point Wild Boar Fell makes its presence known, and will remain the finest feature of the view for some time to come.

Cross the pasture to the base of Cobbles Plantation, then bear left to slant down to join the youthful Ure. Advance upstream to join the drive to Blades at a bridge, and follow this along to the house. Enter the yard and go right to a gate out of it. Note that here a more direct route up to the High Way is available (ese WALK 1). Go immediately left through another gate into a field. Strictly, the right of way bears left across it to a footbridge on the Ure, then doubles sharply back up the pasture, heading directly away to pass through a gate in a fence to locate a corner stile in the wall just behind. Don't look for the two tiny strips of woodland shown on the map, as they don't exist.

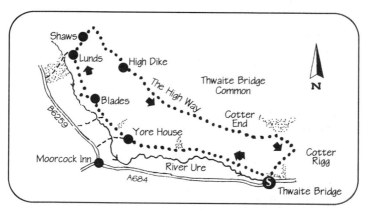

After this messy bit normality resumes. Follow the wall away to the left to another corner stile, then rise up the next field to a stile visible in the wall ahead. Cross the minor brow of Cowshaw Hill to reveal Lunds Chapel below. Descend to it, gaining access via a stile. Lunds Chapel dates from the late 17th century, a very simple old building featuring a bell-cote. A few scattered gravestones still stand, and the view to Wild Boar Fell remains as fine as when the chapel was built.

Pass to a stile behind it and across a stone slab bridge go to a stile into the farmyard. Rise past the house to another stile, then up the field-side to one above. Climb the steep pasture to approach Shaws. This is the former 30-bed youth hostel, opened in 1949. It was the base of the Mallerstang Marathon (the author's first and last organised challenge walk) and a fine 'getaway' spot for walkers and cyclists. Unfashionable perhaps, its demise nevertheless remains a sad loss, particularly now as the inspiring Lady Anne's Way long distance walk virtually passes its door.

Continue up to the right of the ravine in front of it to a bridge over the gill. A flight of steps leads to a gate above the house and alongside further impressive gill scenery. Go left above the confines of Shaws and at the corner, our way is the distinct green rake curving up and tracing a wall up to a stile onto the High Way. From here, the return leg commences with contrastingly simple instructions. Turn right on the track and just stay on it! The way is infallible as it never strays more than a few yards from the company of the attendant wall.

Long strides are matched by long views of high country in this least frequented corner of the National Park. Shortly after High Dike a series of limestone shakeholes and outcrops accompany us. Around this point is a brief appearance of the Howgill Fells between Baugh and Swarth Fells. The High Way is best known as part of the route taken by Lady Anne Clifford when visiting her Westmorland castles in the 17th century. Now a route for more leisurely travellers, it was, for centuries before, the major 'highway' to Kirkby Stephen until the arrival of the turnpike road - the present road turning off at the *Moorcock* - in 1825.

No height is lost (indeed a little is gained) for 2½ miles until arrival at Cotter End. Here the way finally winds down past a fine specimen of a limekiln. Over to the left the mass of Great Shunner Fell slides into place: the skyline presented is the Pennine Way route of ascent. On our left now is the edge of one of the two large coniferous plantations on the flanks of little Cotterdale. Just below is a pair of gates. Take the left one and trace the old way down the wall-side until reaching a stile in the wall. Cross it and bear away, contouring around and down across a track to the top of a slender strip of woodland. From a stile in the wall there slant down again, within yards Thwaite Bridge House appears below. A faint path drops down to a stile into the woods, where a path drops down to return to the start.

*Shaws -
the former
Garsdale Head
Youth Hostel*

4

MOSSDALE & COTTERDALE

START *Appersett*   *Grid ref. SD 858906*

DISTANCE *7¼ miles*

ORDNANCE SURVEY MAPS
1:50,000
Landranger 98 - Wensleydale & Upper Wharfedale
1:25,000
Outdoor Leisure 19 - Howgill Fells/Upper Eden Valley

ACCESS *Start from the green. Park considerately alongside, near the bridge, or just across it. The nearest regular bus service is at Hawes, a mile away.*

Gentle walking through two secluded valleys, with all the major tops around the dalehead on show.

S   Appersett is a small farming community, and the first settlement of such size in Wensleydale. It stands where the waters of Widdale Beck join the main river. **From the green cross the adjacent road bridge over Widdale Beck, and just beyond a barn take a stile on the left. Walk parallel with the road as far as the next bridge (this time over the Ure) but stay in the field and cross a stile to follow the river up-dale.**

On emerging from trees forsake the riverbank and slope up the field: pass along the top of the trees, over a stile and across a hollow to eventually reach a stile into the woods. Drop to cross the stream entering the Ure, then head left to a barn, continuing straight on to join the farm drive going left towards Birk Rigg. Cotter End displays a shapely profile from this neighbourhood.

When the drive turns up to the farm, fork left on another track through the gate in front and accompany it through four further gates. When it swings left to climb through a low scar to Mid Mossdale Farm, leave it and head on to the far end of the field. Now simply follow the river upstream, past a farm bridge to a wedge of trees deflecting us from the Ure. At a gate in the next substantial wall a sketchy track strikes left to the now prominent Mossdale Head Farm.

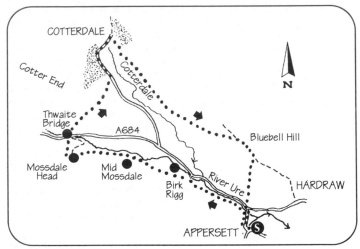

Mossdale is the name given to that stretch of the Ure between Appersett and Mossdale Viaduct. Either side of the viaduct are some lovely falls: its four arches carried the branch line from Hawes to Hawes Junction (now Garsdale Head) on the Settle-Carlisle line. **Pass right of the main building to cross the bridge on Mossdale Beck. Ignore various tracks left and right, and instead climb the field with a wall on the right. At the top go right over a fence-stile and stay near the right-hand wall as the slope steepens to descend to the main road at Thwaite Bridge.**

Cross both road and bridge and head up a path through the trees. From a stile at the top climb the steep pasture to a stile at the top-right corner. Cross over a track and a gentler brow to locate a stile in the long wall climbing the ridge-end. The biggest views of the walk are to be had while crossing this broad ridge under Cotter End, at 1245ft the walk's highest point. **From the stile cross to another wall from where a steady descent - marshy in parts - is made to the unfenced**

road in Cotterdale. Go left along the cul-de-sac road into the hamlet.
Cotterdale stands at the head of its own little valley, sheltered by broad ridges coming down from Lunds Fell (west) and Great Shunner Fell (east). **On approaching the last buildings leave the road by a footbridge, crossing the fields by obvious gap-stiles. A tiny watercourse takes us along a field-bottom, and at a collapsed intervening wall strike left up a pronounced green rake to a stile in the top wall.**

Turn right to trace the wall to a stile by a barn and maintain this level course for a considerable time through an assortment of pastures, sometimes with a wall for company. One colourful enclosure stands head and shoulders above the rest. **After a particularly clear spell the path becomes less distinct beyond the crumbling walls of an extensive fold. At the very end of the pasture rise to a gap-stile, then keep right of a short length of wall on a trod contouring round towards a stile above. From it contour yet again to join a broad track descending to a gate.** From Cotterdale back to the Ure we tread the extensive slopes of Great Shunner Fell, and here on Bluebell Hill we make a brief acquaintance with the Pennine Way. During this last section the three giants on the south side of Wensleydale (Wether, Dodd and Widdale Fells) fill the scene, with Ingleborough sneaking in behind.

Head down the enclosed track but leave at the first gate on the right. Descend by a wall to a stile, then head down to the far end of a large field. Shortly after the gate use a more prominent gate in the right-hand wall, then aim for a stile in front of roadsigns which indicate arrival at the Hardraw junction of the A684. Go left on the main road, over Ure Bridge and re-entering Appersett as the walk began.

Thwaite Bridge

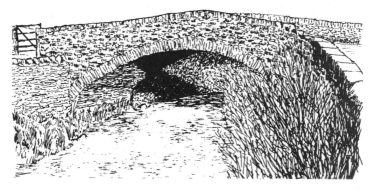

5

AYSGILL FORCE

START Hawes   Grid ref. SD 875898

DISTANCE 3½ miles

ORDNANCE SURVEY MAPS
1:50,000
Landranger 98 - Wensleydale & Upper Wharfedale
1:25,000
Outdoor Leisure 2 - Yorkshire Dales West **or**
Outdoor Leisure 30 - Yorkshire Dales North/Central

ACCESS Start from the National Park car park in the old station yard.
Hawes is served by bus from Leyburn.

A stroll in the valley of Gayle Beck, visiting one of Wensleydale's
lesser known waterfalls.

S   For notes on Hawes please refer to page 24. **Leave through the
small main street car park almost opposite the *Board Inn*. From a stile
in its left corner a sketchy path rises half-right across two fields to
join the Gayle road. Turn left past the creamery into the heart of the
village.**

The Wensleydale Creamery is a long established business that was on
the verge of disappearing in 1992, along with many jobs. Happily a
management buyout has hopefully secured its future, and enterpris-
ing plans have seen its popularity soar. Milk from the cows you will
see on your walk is used in the production of the celebrated Wensleydale cheese. From watching the cows munch the grass to nibbling the
finished product, you can enjoy the whole experience! Synonymous
with the creamery is the name of Kit Calvert, a local farmer and
archetypal Dalesman whose remarkable efforts saved the business
over half a century earlier.

The delightful village of Gayle was here long before its big brother came on the scene. Solid stone cottages fan out along lanes from the little arched bridge, on either side of which Gayle Beck tumbles over a series of ledges.

After leaning on the bridge take the short, cobbled way to the right, continuing along the lane to a kissing-gate after the last house on the left. Climb half-right past a wall corner to a stile, and continue at the same angle to a stile above the beck before descending to its bank. The way is now straightforward, shadowing Gayle Beck upstream to Aysgill Force, deep in a wooded dell.

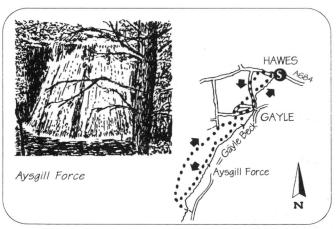

Aysgill Force

Above the falls follow the beck past two footbridges, the second by a barn. At the end of the next field leave the beck by rising right to join a farm track at a gate. This green track doubles back to the right, becoming enclosed and eventually gaining a solid surface. Just a little further, after a bend, a stile on the right commences our tracing of the Pennine Way. Two fields are crossed to a stile used earlier in the walk, turning left to shadow a wall down onto a lane. Almost immediately take a lane joining it to descend to the edge of Gayle.

The PW skirts the centre by branching left across two fields, passing between modern housing to debouch onto the Hawes road. Go briefly left then leave the road at a barn on the right. A flagged path runs above Gayle Beck to arrive at the parish church. Either branch of the fork will deposit you back onto the main street.

6

HARDRAW FORCE

START *Hawes*   *Grid ref. SD 875898*

DISTANCE *7¼ miles*

ORDNANCE SURVEY MAPS
1:50,000
Landranger 98 - Wensleydale & Upper Wharfedale
1:25,000
Outdoor Leisure 30 - Yorkshire Dales North/Central

ACCESS *Start from the National Park car park in the old station yard.
Hawes is served by bus from Leyburn.*

A superbly varied walk with extensive views across Wensleydale.

S Hawes is the 'capital' of upper Wensleydale, a lively, colourful
market town to which all visitors are drawn. The place gains even
greater character at its Tuesday market, when there are, happily, as
many locals in evidence as tourists. An unconventional layout includes some cobbled road, and a leisurely exploration is really
essential. Places of interest include the parish church of St. Margaret
dating from 1851; a modern youth hostel on this major staging post
on the Pennine Way; and a celebrated antiquarian bookshop.

Once the last stop on the Wensleydale branch line, Hawes station has
been put to use as a National Park Centre. Also keeping the station
yard alive is the Dales Countryside Museum, where one can learn of
local life and industry of the not so distant past. Two surviving
industries are today also tourist attractions. The absorbing ropemakers
is at the old station entrance, and you can observe and purchase any
number of associated products. The creamery is found on the Gayle
road, and described more in WALK 5.

From the car park a path rises by the old railway bridge up onto the road. Turn right to follow it out of town. Within yards a drive heads off left, and with it a gate signals the route of the Pennine Way. Its flagged course is followed to rejoin the road a little further. Cross Haylands Bridge on the Ure then take a stile which soon appears on the right, a sketchy path crossing the field to a small arched bridge.

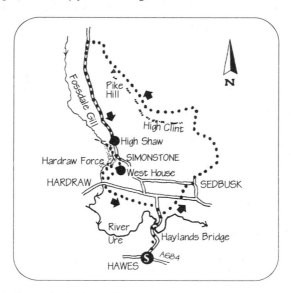

From it the path climbs half-right to a stile, from where a large field is crossed to a stile in the top corner. Cross straight over the road to a stile opposite, and resume the rise in the same direction. Two further stiles quickly ensue before a near-vertical climb to another stile in the top-right corner. Turn right along the road to the hamlet of Sedbusk. This unspoilt hamlet of farms and cottages looks across the dale to Hawes and beyond from an altitude little under 1000 feet. It is so laid back it has even avoided the back road from Hardraw to Askrigg, being reached only by a narrow lane. Entering its confines, note the old Primitive Methodist Chapel of 1875, now a private house.

Head up the lane between the houses, and at the top end of the small green bear right as the lane deteriorates into a rough track. This is Shutt Lane, which slants up the hillside to be vacated by a stile on the left just before a gate. A good sunken track works its way up the field, passing a tiny plantation and then slanting left to a gate. The track runs on to another gate which gives access to the open fell.

Continue straight up the track keeping left of a low scar, and the way then gives High Clint, on the left, a wide berth before swinging round onto the plateau, meeting up there with a more attractive path that has stayed with High Clint's escarpment: a prominent cairn to the left overlooks a splendid group of stone men. The walk reaches its highest point of 1750ft on this plateau. From these northern slopes of the dale we enjoy extensive panoramas over upper Wensleydale. Rising above Hawes are those ubiquitous 2000-footers Wether Fell, Dodd Fell and Widdale Fell. The road to Wharfedale over Fleet Moss (1934ft) is also clearly in sight.

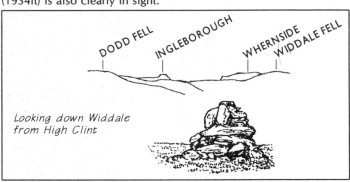

DODD FELL   INGLEBOROUGH   WHERNSIDE   WIDDALE FELL

*Looking down Widdale
from High Clint*

Back on the track, a left fork is passed and the way quickly peters out. Forge straight on to another series of cairns on Pike Hill, and maintain a level course to arrive at the lively environs of Shivery Gill. Cross to a track on the other side and turn down it to join the unfenced Buttertubs road, which is now followed downhill for a good 1¼ miles.

At the first farm buildings at High Shaw turn along the lane on the right, only to leave it after a few yards by descending steps to heavily wooded Fossdale Gill. After seeing the waterfall a few yards up, turn to accompany the beck downstream. A footbridge offers a choice of banks, and below two more low falls a second footbridge is reached. Here we must leave the beck to prepare itself for its big moment, to be witnessed from below: a path goes left up to join the road.

Go right for only a minute and leave the road by a stile alongside a gate. A good track heads away and down to West House Farm, and from a stile to its right a path descends two more fields to emerge via a yard into Hardraw. This tiny hamlet is made famous by its waterfall, claimed to be the highest single drop above ground in England. It also has its own little church, St. Mary & St. John (1881) across the bridge.

Access to Hardraw Force is through the *Green Dragon* inn, where a charge is made to view the 'private' spectacle: it is but a 5-minute walk into the increasingly impressive amphitheatre. More so than most, the tiny beck needs to have seen recent rain for the scene to be fully appreciated.

The cliff over which the water spills is Hardraw Scaur, or Scar. In the gorge below the force century-old band contests have made a revival - the old bandstand is passed on the way.

Back at the pub, cross the road and take a track just left of the bridge. Go left behind the buildings to a small gate from where a largely flagged path crosses the fields to eventually join a road. Turn right to pick up the outward route, re-crossing Haylands Bridge and back into Hawes.

Hardraw Force

7

WETHER FELL

START Burtersett   Grid ref. SD 890892

DISTANCE 5¼ miles

ORDNANCE SURVEY MAPS
1:50,000
Landranger 98 - Wensleydale & Upper Wharfedale
1:25,000
Outdoor Leisure 30 - Yorkshire Dales North/Central

ACCESS There is reasonable parking alongside the lane just above the sharp bend at the village head. Leyburn-Hawes buses pass the road-end.

A well-defined climb to a 2000ft summit combined with a bracing stroll along a Roman road.

S Burtersett is a very attractive little village set well back from the valley floor, and also peacefully above the main road through the dale. Most of the dwellings cluster round a rising lane and a tiny green where spring flowers bloom, with two old chapels including a Wesleyan Methodist Chapel of 1870. **From the green at the top of the village, take the 'no through road' branching off the road corner alongside the old chapel. Almost at once it forks, and our track climbs to the left, leaving the last cottage behind and embracing a steep slope. This broad track still serves the farmer, and so remains easy to follow as it scales the hillside, always sloping to the right.**

On gaining equal height with the highly prominent upthrust of Yorburgh just across to the left, ignore a right fork to a gate and continue straight up. Shortly afterwards the nearby wall finally leaves us for good, and the track - briefly a little less clear - crosses level ground to a gateway.

Beyond it the track improves again, winding up the fellside as a sunken green way. Ignoring lesser branches to left and then right, the track arrives at the last gate of the climb. Ahead, set considerably well back, is the summit of Wether Fell, but the track heading directly out to it should be treated with contempt: within five minutes it will entice the hapless walker into dark, deep peat groughs - definitely not recommended.

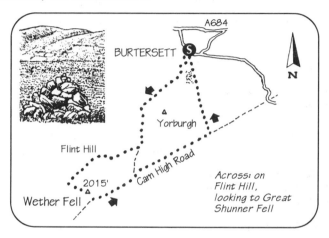

A684

BURTERSETT **S**

N

Yorburgh

Flint Hill

Cam High Road

2015'

Wether Fell

Across: on Flint Hill, looking to Great Shunner Fell

Instead then, accompany the wall along to the right, passing an old quarry on Flint Hill and being greeted by new views across to the west. This rather more circuitous course should not be hastily abandoned: our thin path is heading ever nearer the top, and the temptation to strike out to the left is best avoided until the slope there becomes invitingly steep. At the same time as this our wallside way becomes marshier, less obvious and generally less appealing. Climbing the grass to the left a few peat groughs are encountered at the top, and now the summit cairn appears only a couple of minutes beyond. A level grassy stroll completes a relatively dry ascent.

Wether Fell is a rare venture for us, a climb to 2000 feet. This 'rush of blood' is due to the ease by which this fell can be conquered: Wensleydale's other mountains are set much further back from the valley and constitute a far greater challenge. The summit is known as Drumaldrace, and is probably as good a viewpoint for the Dales mountains as anywhere.

To begin the return journey head down the only drop of any significance to join the broad track of the Cam High Road just to the south. The Cam High Road is the Roman road that lead from Ribblehead to the fort at Bainbridge. The whole of that section forms an exhilarating high-level march that can still be trodden today. Wether Fell is one of two 2000-foot summits it skirts, and here it comes almost within a stone's throw of the top. This renders Wether Fell highly accessible and ensures a near-foolproof route of escape in bad weather. Though 'improved' further westward, several miles still remain to provide a gem of a traffic-free route for the walker. **The old road is now followed for quite a distance on its gentle descent eastwards to Bainbridge, soon becoming enclosed by walls. The point of departure from it is about a mile beyond this, where a footpath sign at a stile indicates the way to Burtersett.**

Summit cairn, Wether Fell

A slender green path slopes down to a stile from where a path slanting right is ignored in favour of the thinner one straight ahead. The path improves during a pleasant, direct descent of the large pasture to a stile just left of a wall corner. Just a few yards over the brow Burtersett reveals itself, and the way is obvious through the final fields of the descent: from the bottom corner of a woeful plantation a trio of stiles precedes emergence onto the road in Burtersett.

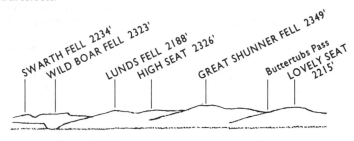

SWARTH FELL 2234'
WILD BOAR FELL 2323'
LUNDS FELL 2188'
HIGH SEAT 2326'
GREAT SHUNNER FELL 2349'
Buttertubs Pass
LOVELY SEAT 2215'

Looking north-west from Wether Fell to the mountains of Mallerstang and upper Wensleydale

8

SEMERWATER

START Semerwater   Grid ref. SD 921875

DISTANCE 4 miles

ORDNANCE SURVEY MAPS
1:50,000
Landranger 98 - Wensleydale & Upper Wharfedale
1:25,000
Outdoor Leisure 30 - Yorkshire Dales North/Central

ACCESS Start from the lake foreshore near the bridge. Fee payable at Low Blean - see signs.

A very easy circuit of Semerwater, the largest lake in the old North Riding of Yorkshire. In a district not over endowed with sheets of water it has become a popular venue for a variety of water sports, and an association exists to control the activities and help protect bird life. Near the lakefoot is the Carlow Stone, once dropped by a giant. The best known legend of the district relates how a visitor, inhospitably treated, caused a whole 'city' to disappear under the waters. What seems a little more certain is that Iron age lake dwellings existed here.

S **From the foreshore head along the road away from the bridge (not over it), and at the foot of the hill - just opposite Low Blean Farm - take a stile on the right. Maintain a level course through the fields, taking in several stiles to emerge close to the lakeshore. By this time a good path has materialised, and it heads gradually upwards across the rough pastures above the head of the lake.**

More stiles ensue before arriving at the remains of Stalling Busk's old chapel. A stile is provided to enable a look round the ruin, which stands in strange isolation some 200 feet below the hamlet. Originally dating from 1603, it was rebuilt in 1722 and replaced by the new church in 1909. The ruins romantically overlook the lake, and exude an atmosphere not felt at the replacement St. Matthews up by the houses. **Only yards beyond it the barely evident path forks. Head up to the left on an improving path alongside a small beck: this old churchgoers' way leads unerringly up onto the cul-de-sac road through Stalling Busk.**

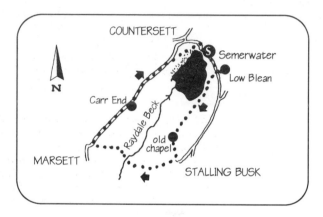

Walk only a few yards to the right through the hamlet, and before a sharp bend take the rough track of Busk Lane down to the right. This enclosed way runs down to a ford on Cragdale Water, then heads away, forsaking it at a bend - by a footbridge - to cross two lesser becks directly ahead: this neighbourhood is usually rather moist. Beyond, the track soon becomes enclosed to enter Marsett alongside Marsett Beck.

The side valley containing Semerwater has no satisfactory name, though Semerdale has sometimes been offered as a makeshift title. Above the lake it is generally referred to as Raydale, this being the central, largest and only level one of the three valleys which merge between Marsett and Stalling Busk. Bardale and Cragdale are the lesser two. Both Marsett and Stalling Busk are peaceful farming hamlets, largely untouched even by the tourists that frequent Semerwater, even less those down in the main valley. Marsett in the valley bottom and Stalling Busk perched on the hillside with good views of the lake.

The Carlow Stone, Semerwater

Cross the green to the road bridge, and follow the quiet, generally level road for approximately one and a third miles. Shortly after a brief climb, journey's end beckons at the lakefoot, and as the lane descends take a stile into a field on the right. Accompany a tiny beck down to a gate, then crossing the beck to contend with a short, muddy walk through the trees. A gate admits onto the road at Semerwater Bridge, which is now crossed to complete the circuit.

The old chapel,
Stalling Busk

9

THE RIVER BAIN & ROMAN ROAD

START Bainbridge   Grid ref. SD 933901

DISTANCE 5¾ miles

ORDNANCE SURVEY MAPS
1:50,000
Landranger 98 - Wensleydale & Upper Wharfedale
1:25,000
Outdoor Leisure 30 - Yorkshire Dales North/Central

ACCESS Start in the village centre. Ample parking alongside the greens. Bainbridge is served by Hawes-Leyburn buses.

A steady ramble by the shortest river and along an ancient highway, with Semerwater sandwiched in between.

S Bainbridge is a lovely village whose houses stand well back from an enormous green. Though the main road cuts across, its effect seems insignificant. The most noticeable features are the stocks which still grace the green, and the whitewashed *Rose & Crown* which is always in sight. It dates back several centuries and is possibly the oldest pub in the dale. The structure which gives the village its name is itself several centuries old, having been widened in 1785. It is a shapely platform from which to see not only the best stretch of the river, but the only part before it sneaks quietly round the backs of the houses.

The village has notable historical connections, not least of all with Romans. Brough Hill, peering over the houses at the east end of the village, is the site of the Roman fort *Braccium* and a handy place to defend, which was no doubt just as well. Centuries later the Norman lords based their foresters here, when the Forest of Wensleydale was a popular hunting ground. At the inn can be seen a horn, blown at nine o'clock in winter months to guide benighted travellers to safety. Its origin goes back earlier, as a warning sound in the days of the forest. The event survives purely as a quaint custom. Where our walk re-enters the village is a house that was once the Old Dame School, where over a century ago, pupils could learn the 'three R's' for 2d a week (that's 1p to you youngsters!). There is a former Independent Chapel of 1864 with bell and clock still in place, the old school of 1875 on the green, a Temperance Hall of 1910, a Post office/store, toilets and a tearoom. Near the pub is a house with a 1670 datestone.

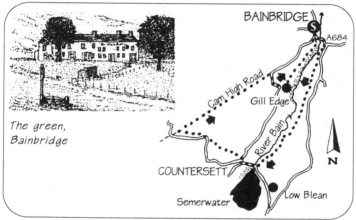

The green, Bainbridge

Leave Bainbridge by the main road to Aysgarth at the corner of the green, crossing the bridge over the river Bain and climbing the steep hill. Take a stile on the right just before a junction and head across the pasture, keeping well above the steep drop to the river. Pass to the left of an 'island' field and at the brow of the hill a sketchy path leads on to a stile. Marker posts show the way down the slope beyond, with Semerwater now fully in view ahead.

Head on through stiles in the intervening walls, and at a ladder-stile bear right to finally join up with the now adjacent riverbank. Its pleasant course offers a simple walk upstream to quickly arrive at the road at Semerwater Bridge. Joining the Ure at Bainbridge the river Bain is claimed to be the shortest in the country, a point which the Dibb in Wharfedale would challenge. Our route explores it comprehensively, from the numerous falls over rock ledges above Bainbridge to its so tranquil meander from Semerwater Bridge.

Before crossing the bridge have a potter along the lakeshore itself. Semerwater was the largest lake in the North Riding of Yorkshire, and in an area not lavishly endowed with sheets of water it has become a popular venue for a variety of watersports. An association exists to control these activities and help protect birdlife. Near the lakefoot is the mighty Carlow Stone, said to have been dropped by a giant. The best known legend of the district relates how a visitor, inhospitably treated, caused a whole 'city' to be submerged under the waters. What is more certain is that Iron age lake dwellings existed here.

Resume by crossing the bridge to climb the steep road to a cross-roads at Countersett. This small hamlet has an early Friends' Meeting House and a lovely old hall dating from 1650 (see page 1), also with strong Quaker connections. The steep slopes above command a superb panorama of Semerwater's side-valley. The best feature is Addlebrough across the valley. **Turn right for the hamlet, but just before the first house opt instead for an enclosed track to some cottages on the left. Taking a gate by the first dwelling on the left, begin a steep climb to first one and then a second barn. From it rise half-left to a stile and continue diagonally up to the wall rising to the far corner.** At this point the Semerwater scene is finally left behind.

From the stile follow the wall up to a gate onto the Countersett-Burtersett road at its highest point. At 1375ft this is also the summit of the walk. **Go right for a couple of minutes to reach a stile on the right. A sketchy path crosses a collapsed wall and then fades in rough pasture as it slants down to a stile onto the Cam High Road.** This is the Roman road running from Ribblehead to Bainbridge. On this walk we tread the easternmost section which points itself unerringly at Bainbridge. Even in this lower stretch which is stony underfoot but not rough, the views are very good. An unrivalled length of Wensleydale can be seen, including Hawes, Askrigg, various individual features and most of the surrounding fells. Looking back up the road, Wether Fell and its outcrop Yorburgh are seen at their shapeliest.

Turn right to follow the arrow-like course of the Roman road until eventual hi-jack by a modern road. Head up this road as far as Gill Edge, just ahead, and turn along its drive. From a stile on the left descend to one at the field bottom, from where a sketchy path crosses two fields to a barn. A clearer path runs on to two further stiles, and from a gate above the river descends the wall-side to the edge of Bainbridge. The path becomes enclosed to run past cottages before re-emerging onto the village green.

ADDLEBROUGH

START Worton   Grid ref. SD 958899

DISTANCE 6½ miles

ORDNANCE SURVEY MAPS
1:50,000
Landranger 98 - Wensleydale & Upper Wharfedale
1:25,000
Outdoor Leisure 30 - Yorkshire Dales North/Central

ACCESS Start from the pub on the Aysgarth road out of the village. There is a spacious lay-by opposite, beyond the patrons' parking. Served by Leyburn-Aysgarth-Hawes buses.

A straightforward circuit of a shapely fell, with outstanding views.

S Worton is only a small collection of dwellings along the main valley road, but still manages a pub of its own, the *Victoria* (with 1698 datestone), and a grand old house in the shape of Worton Hall, with mullioned windows. Note also a house dated 1729 bearing an inscription above a side window: *'MICHAEL SMITH MECHANICK BUT HE THAT BUILT ALL THINGS IS GOD Heb 3'.* Worton is separated from Askrigg by the Ure's most uninteresting bridge.

From the lay-by head past the pub to the first road junction, and turn up the steep lane to Cubeck. Turn into the farming hamlet and then immediately left up a steep, rough lane. At a gate the track runs more freely, sloping across a field and then up to a gate at the top corner. Here Addleborough makes its first appearance. **Behind the gate the track fades: cross to a gate over to the right after which the way picks up again to resume its level course. From the next gate it accompanies a wall away to emerge onto the quiet road to Carpley Green.**

Turn left along its traffic-free course, leaving it only on approaching the first barn at the farm. Carpley Green stands at the end of the road as far as motor traffic is concerned, but an old packhorse way continues over the Stake to the Kidstones Pass and Wharfedale, a splendid route for walkers and cyclists. **From a gate on the left follow a wall through a field to a gate giving access to a large pasture on Addlebrough's upper flank. A raised green way sets the course as it rakes across, bearing a little to the right, and then continuing on through a natural pass around the back of Addlebrough.**

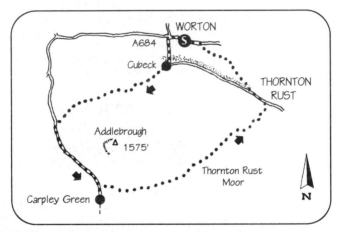

Addlebrough is a classic table-topped fell that seems to crop up in almost every Wensleydale view. Modest crags line its northern side and help to accentuate the abrupt edge of the plateau. The Iron age Brigante tribe is thought to have occupied a hillfort here - no doubt in stark contrast to the Roman fort in the valley bottom. It should be noted that our route does not take in Addlebrough's summit as it is bereft of rights of way and walls intervene. It is hard, however, to deny oneself a brief diversion, free of walls, to the rocky scarp above: it offers splendid views including a bird's-eye picture of an Iron age settlement near the top; even to the untrained eye it is obvious. The undoubted highlight is the view of Semerwater in its deep bowl of fells.

After two intervening walls the way finally links up with that right-hand wall and succumbs to a gate in it. An improving grassy track surmounts the modest ridge, and beyond a stile the expanse of

Thornton Rust Moor is now firmly underfoot. Towards the bottom of Thornton Rust Moor much of the lower dale comes back into view, while behind us, Addlebrough's familiar outline returns yet again. **Our splendid track strikes half-left across undulating terrain, leaving the moor at a gate from where the walled confines of Moor Lane channel us unerringly down into Thornton Rust.** This lovely village is strung along a quiet lane, and like many others in the dale is free from the bustle of the valley floor. It includes a mission attached to Aysgarth church, an Institute of 1924 and a number of attractive houses.

Addlebrough from Moor Lane

Go left along the road to the edge of the village, and just past a cottage garden take a second small gate on the right, labelled Nipe End. From a stile below, a path runs through slender woodland to emerge into a field. Here the final leg begins, a pathless trek through green pastures linked by a fine collection of stiles. The only potentially confusing one is the first, found in the crumbling wall half-left of our emergence from the trees. This sets the general course for delivery onto the main road: the start is along to the left.

The Victoria Arms, Worton

39

AROUND ASKRIGG

START Askrigg   Grid ref. SD 948910

DISTANCE 7 miles

ORDNANCE SURVEY MAPS
1:50,000
Landranger 98 - Wensleydale & Upper Wharfedale
1:25,000
Outdoor Leisure 30 - Yorkshire Dales North/Central

ACCESS Start from the village centre. Reasonable parking. Askrigg is served by Leyburn-Hawes buses.

A richly varied walk of which the highlights are two superb waterfalls. This walk embraces such contrasting attractions that one may feel to be not doing justice to everything. More so than most the walk lends itself to being divided into two shorter rambles, using the Muker road as the link.

S Askrigg is a wonderfully different village, seeming of another age to the 'typical' Dales village. Formerly a market town and a famous clockmaking centre, Askrigg gradually gave way to Hawes as centre for the upper dale. The heart of the village still recalls those days: the market cross of 1830, the three-storeyed houses along the main street and 15th century St. Oswald's church. Most striking feature internally is the roof with its splendid old beams; the font is probably a good 500 years old, and bears the marks of hinges from the 17th century days when it was locked to prevent theft of Holy Water for Black Magic rites! There is a Post office/store and two pubs, the *Crown* and the *Kings Arms*. The latter is attached to the Manor House, and is dated 1767. Rising directly across the valley, flat-topped Addlebrough is prominent in the Askrigg scene.

Follow the main road in the Hawes direction out of the bottom end of the village, and after the last house on the left take a track down the near side of an animal feeds works. From the gate at the bottom pass between the supports of a former railway bridge and continue in the same direction through a series of stiles.

From the final stile a path heads straight on for the river, but instead of following it to the very bank, go left on a low embankment to a stile in a wall corner. Follow the fence away from it (parallel with the Ure) to a stile by a gate, from where the riverbank is finally gained. Now accompany the Ure downstream to soon emerge onto a road adjacent to the characterless Worton Bridge. Our brief meeting with the Ure finds it in predictably calm mood.

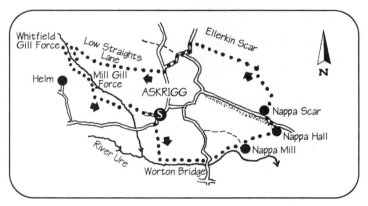

Without crossing the bridge, continue down-river from a stile opposite. After a pair of footbridges in rapid succession a gate brings arrival at Nappa Mill Farm. Take the farm road up to the left, but leave it by a stile on the right just before crossing the beck at an attractive corner. Climb diagonally away on a green track up to the right-hand of two gates, and continue in the same direction to a gate admitting to the environs of Nappa Hall.

Nappa Hall dates from the 15th century, a fortified manor house of the influential Metcalfe family. It now operates as a farm. In season a stunning display of snowdrops carpets the immediate wooded neighbourhood. **Follow the enclosed track up past the farm buildings and out onto the road.**

Turn left along the road only as far as the first branch right, signposted 'no through road', and head up through the hamlet of Nappa Scar. Remain on this lane which at the top of the hill becomes roughly surfaced. The views now become very extensive, the fells on the south side of the valley ranging from Penhill to Addlebrough, and Wether, Dodd and Widdale Fells. The track swings left for a long and pleasurable level march to debouch onto a narrow road climbing out of Askrigg. Turn down towards the valley, ignoring in turn a road left, a track right, and then a road right (to Muker). Just below is another walled track, and this we follow along to the right.

Nappa Hall

Remain on this rough way known as Low Straights Lane to its very terminus, and here escape by a stile on the left: Whitfield Gill Force at once makes its presence known through the trees directly below. Our route must take a circuitous course in order to stand at its foot, for the steep slopes deter a direct descent. Instead the path heads downstream high above the wooded beck before dropping to a footbridge, then rises to meet the path to the waterfall. Turning upstream, care is needed as the final yards can be slippery underfoot. The scene is worth the effort however, for this is a spectacular plunge into an impending amphitheatre. Though not as tall as the better known Hardraw Force just up-dale, some of its aspects rate it finer, not least of all the fact that it's free!

To resume the walk retrace steps to the junction and keep straight on to a stile. From here on the original footpath spent much time outside the wooded confines of the gill, but a thoughtfully created replacement has provided us with a more intimate route. After a stile beyond a sidestream some time is still spent outside the boundary wall, but the path is soon returned to the action after the second of two sections in the fields.

The return path runs once more along the top of the steep, wooded bank, and at a junction the detour to our second waterfall is made: the situation is a near-replica of the one experienced further up the beck. This time, however, it is but a brief stroll along a much firmer path upstream to witness the delights of the equally impressive waterfall of Mill Gill Force. Although the two waterfalls occupy similar settings in deep wooded gorges, their characters are vastly different. The first is a straight drop, the latter a staircase of ledges.

After admiring the cascades return to the junction of paths and continue downstream on an excellent path on the top side of the wooded gill. The bonus of a distant view across Wensleydale is now added to the charms of the gill itself. At the bottom of the wood a brace of neighbouring stiles point the way to a small footbridge on the beck.

Just downstream of the footbridge our track parts company with the beck to pass to the left of a former mill and under a simple aqueduct to a stile. A neat, flagged path runs from here across the field to join a lane, which runs along to the left to re-enter Askrigg.

Whitfield Gill Force

Mill Gill Force

12

IVY SCAR & CARPERBY

START Aysgarth   Grid ref. SE 011887

DISTANCE 7¼ miles

ORDNANCE SURVEY MAPS
1:50,000
Landranger 98 - Wensleydale & Upper Wharfedale
1:25,000
Outdoor Leisure 30 - Yorkshire Dales North/Central

ACCESS Start from the National Park car park at Aysgarth Falls, east of the village. Aysgarth is served by Leyburn-Hawes buses.

Easy walking and sharp contrasts between riverbank and hillside.

S   Aysgarth is made famous by its series of Upper, Middle and Lower Falls. Here the Yoredale series of limestone rocks make their greatest showing to create a water wonderland. It is the grand scale of things rather than their height that provides the spectacle. What makes all this truly beautiful is the setting - thickly wooded with rich plant life.

Leave the car park at the opposite end to the entrance to find a well-used footpath leading down to Yore Bridge, viewpoint for the Upper Falls. Yore Bridge is a gracefully tall single-span structure. Originally from the 16th century, it has since been much widened. Yore of course is the older name for the river Ure. The large building adjacent to the bridge is Yore Mill, a former spinning mill which houses the Yorkshire Carriage Museum.

Climb the steep road as far as the church drive. St. Andrew's church is a magnificent place of worship with many fine features: go take a look and see also the notes at the foot of page 51. Just up the hill are a pub, the *Palmer Flatt Hotel,* and the youth hostel which closed in 2004. **Take a stile across the road from where an intermittent way**

runs across the fields, keeping generally level and squeezing through a multitude of identical gap-stiles on this villagers' church path. On the edge of Aysgarth the way becomes enclosed to join a back lane, which leads up to the Methodist chapel on the edge of the village green.

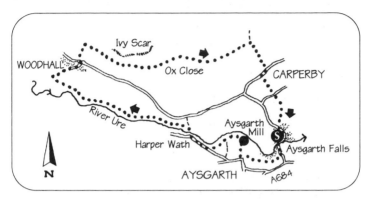

Aysgarth village stands high above the river, entirely aloof from the natural attraction that brings visitors in their tens of thousands. There is a spacious air about the place, and a green flanks the main road which divides the rows of houses. Village pub is the *George & Dragon*, while there is also a tearoom, Post office/store, pottery, war memorial, and stocks on the second green. **The point of arrival is also the point of departure, through a narrow gap between houses on the right. A path descends through two stiles and down alongside a wall, using a stile in it to cross half-right before arriving at the former Aysgarth Mill. A stile on its left deposits us onto its access track, which is followed along to the left.**

When the track turns to climb the hill, leave it by a stile on the right: beyond a barn another stile gives access to a pleasant path through trees by the riverside, emerging to continue on to a stile where road and river converge. Head on along the road for a very short distance to Harper Wath, where a long, narrow footbridge conveys us across the Ure.

A stile on the left marks the commencement of a long, easy stretch along the quiet riverbank. This pathless trek clings to the river to become temporarily confined in a rough section between an old

railway embankment and the Ure. On emerging remain with the wall, crossing a small beck as the wall parts company before reaching a stile. Continue on to the next stile to join an enclosed farm track, and turn up beneath a former railway bridge. The improved lane rises up through the hamlet of Woodhall and out onto the Carperby-Askrigg road. Strung along its short lane, the hamlet of Woodhall is almost hidden in a surround of greenery, and appropriately enough it has connections with the old hunting forest of Wensleydale.

Ivy Scar from Woodhall

Cross straight over and pass between house and barns opposite to take a farm track up the steep field. Towards the top of the steep section opt for the right branch to the gate just ahead. The day's climbing is now complete, and a good, level track runs along to the right, through a gate to a ford at the top of Disher Force. While there is no right of way, a brief detour through the gate just before the ford provides a first-class view of this fine waterfall.

Disher Force

From a gate behind the ford, our track (Oxclose Road, a former miners' track) heads across Ox Close Pasture to the old lead mines under the tilted cliff of Ivy Scar. Ox Close has seen its share of activity in days past. The remains of a lead mine are there for all to see, while by the path is the site of a hut circle, 30 yards in diameter. Weaving through spoil heaps the track emerges at the far end to continue on its way a little sketchily. Eventually arriving at a gate, swing right to a gate - the second on the right - in the far corner, descending similarly a cart track through another field.

In this enclosure we pass the remains of an old quarry where the hard flagstone was mined for roofing slates. **The track falls to a gate on the right, continuing down through two fields. Half-way down the second locate a stile on the left, and cross a field bottom to another stile. Descend the narrow enclosure to gates by farm buildings to emerge onto the road in Carperby.**

Carperby is one of the most attractive and least spoilt villages in the dale. Its depth is virtually non-existant, for all its sturdy stone dwellings line the road running through the village. Standing well back from the valley bottom, it was once of greater importance as testified by the sizeable market cross. Dating from the 17th century it stands at one end of the narrow green. At the opposite end is a good grouping of chapels which have sadly been succumbing to modern trends: these include a Methodist chapel of 1820 and a Friends' Meeting House of 1864. It is said the Wensleydale breed of sheep was first named here.

— Yore Bridge, Aysgarth Falls —

Turn left along the main street as far as the *Wheatsheaf Inn*, and take a gate opposite to enter a slender field in between houses. Keep on as far as a stile on the right, then continue on through a similar field to emerge via a stile onto a farm road, Low Lane. Cross straight over and follow a wall away to a stile on the right. From it an intermittent path strikes half-right through several fields, with a string of traditional gap-stiles serving to confirm the way.

Before long the path enters an attractive pocket of woodland: cross straight over the main track through it, and a path leads half-right down onto a road. Turn left, under the old railway bridge, and the falls car park is immediately on the right. To round off the walk in style, a gate just across the road gives speedy access to the Middle Falls. The Lower Falls can also be added by continuing on the main woodland path downstream.

13

BISHOPDALE VILLAGES

START *Aysgarth*   *Grid ref. SE 011887*

DISTANCE *7 miles*

ORDNANCE SURVEY MAPS
1:50,000
Landranger 98 - Wensleydale & Upper Wharfedale
1:25,000
Outdoor Leisure 30 - Yorkshire Dales North/Central

ACCESS *Start from the National Park car park at Aysgarth Falls, east of the village. Aysgarth is served by Leyburn-Hawes buses.*

A gentle walk around the villages based at the foot of Bishopdale, linked by delightful fieldpaths around the base of declining ridges, culminating in a dramatic arrival on the quiet side of Aysgarth Falls.

S   Aysgarth is made famous by its series of Upper, Middle and Lower Falls. Here the Yoredale series of limestone rocks make their greatest showing to create a water wonderland. It is the grand scale of things rather than their height that provides the spectacle. What makes all this truly beautiful is the setting - thickly wooded with rich plant life.

Leave the car park at the opposite end to the entrance to find a well-used footpath leading down to Yore Bridge, viewpoint for the Upper Falls. Yore Bridge is a graceful, single-span structure. Originally 16th century, it has since been much widened. Yore of course is the older name for the river Ure. Adjacent to the bridge is Yore Mill, a former spinning mill which now houses the Yorkshire Carriage Museum.

Climb the steep road as far as the church drive. We shall pass through the churchyard at the walk's end. Just up the hill is a pub, the *Palmer Flatt Hotel,* and the youth hostel which closed in 2004. **Take a stile**

across the road from where an intermittent way runs across the fields, keeping generally level and squeezing through a multitude of identical gap-stiles on this villagers' church path. On the edge of Aysgarth the way becomes enclosed to join a back lane, which leads up to a Methodist chapel on the edge of the village green. Aysgarth stands high above the river, aloof from the natural attraction that brings visitors in their hordes. There is a spacious air about the place, and a green flanks the main road which divides the rows of houses. Village pub is the *George & Dragon*, while there is also a tearoom, Post office/store, pottery, and a war memorial and stocks.

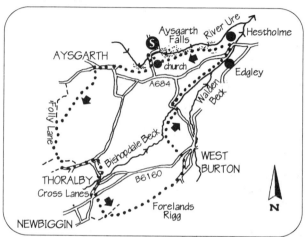

Head along the main street to where the road drops out of the village and remain on the Thornton Rust road. Leave almost at once by a stile and snicket on the left between houses. Into a field, rise up the wall-side to be joined by a track. Continue up until it emerges into a field and promptly fades. Don't advance to the barn ahead but cross to a gap-stile on the right. Slant left up past a barn to another stile, then turn right along the wall-side. Over to the left is Penhill, with views back to Ivy Scar, Bolton Castle and the moors above.

A series of such stiles send the invisible path off, gently curving left as they go. At the fourth bear more sharply over to a gateway towards the far end, then on to a gate/stile alongside a barn. Cross a trickle of a stream and up to a gap-stile behind, then bear left to a gap-stile near the far end again. A faint way crosses a corner of rough pasture to the next stile, where turn sharp right to follow the wall onto Folly Lane. Turn left on this good green way, which sadly lives up to its name as it quickly drops to a sudden and ignominious end at a ford on Heaning Gill.

From the gate behind rise up a part-sunken old way to a gate. Bear right over the brow of this large field, passing through a long-abandoned wall. Here are grand views across to Penhill and up Bishopdale to Forelands Rigg. The exit is hidden in a dip on the other side. Here Thoralby appears below. A firm track forms to go down through the gate/stile, soon joining another track, Haw Lane. Go left down this to emerge into Thoralby. Note that a branch right part-way down gives a chance to see the old hall at Town Head with its 1641 dated lintel before going left into the village.

Thoralby is a pleasant, less touristy village than many of its Wensley-dale counterparts. It retains its pub, the *George*, and features some very attractive old cottages and a neat triangular green. At the central junction is a former Methodist chapel of 1888, and next to the Post office/store a memorial hall of 1887.

Just past the shop turn right down a very minor lane. This quickly expires and a pathway runs on over a stream (ford and slab bridge) to emerge at Low Green. Easiest way is to turn right here for the road, then left for Mill Bridge. Alternatively bear left along this minor lane. Within yards take a stile on the right, on through the tiniest snicket then across step-stiles in several new fences and on to join the road at the converted mill. Go left down to Mill Bridge on Bishopdale Beck and right to join the B6160 at Cross Lanes. The building alongside is an outdoor centre; just up to the right is the *Street Head Inn*, while along the minor road opposite is the hamlet of Newbiggin.

Our way goes left a few yards along the main road, to a gap-stile on the right. Head up by a hedge and tiny stream, and continue up two further fields to a corner stile onto Ox Pasture Lane. Take the stile opposite and then contour left across the field to a prominent stile. From here on the way is clearly and regularly punctuated by a line of stiles, each being visible from the previous one. In time a barn is reached on a little ridge. Go right to a tiny stream and resume in its company, a track forming to quickly enter Town Head at West Burton by way of a farmyard. Advance down the full length of the village. For more on West Burton please refer to WALK 15.

Keep left at the shop, and as the road becomes enclosed go down until a gate sends a short-lived way between houses on the left. This drops down onto the B6160. From a gate almost opposite cross the field centre to the barn ahead. From the gate to its left bear right to the far end to join the beck, down a few yards to the next stile then cross to a wall-end by the beck, then away with the wall. At an intervening stile cross straight over the field past a football pitch to a stile onto the road by Eshington Bridge, built in 1883.

Cross the bridge and turn immediately downstream. This time we cling to the beck, soon passing through Westholme caravan site. Features en route are, at the far end of the site, a tree sporting a quite remarkable girth; a little further, we pass the attractive confluence of Bishopdale and Walden Becks; two follies can also be seen over to the right. Beyond a farm footbridge we are deflected left to a stile onto the A684. Go right for a couple of minutes to approach Hestholme Bridge, but without crossing turn off left at Hestholme's drive. Immediately take a stile on the left and cross to the far corner. Here we gain a high wooded bank above the Ure.

Turn upstream, soon dropping almost to the very water's edge. This is a delectable corner, with a long, low waterfall being a charming prelude to Aysgarth's Lower Falls. At the second enclosure in the river's company the path is deflected up above the craggy, wooded bank that is forming, and we run on higher above again. As we pass through stile and gate in partnership, there are splendid views of the crashing Lower Falls below our bank of stately beeches. The path is deflected higher above a steeper bank by a crumbling wall, and with the Middle Falls and Aysgarth church tower visible, bear left from the highest point of the bank to the left corner of a wood across the field. A stile leads to a path running through it. Emerging at the other end, the church is neatly framed just ahead. Cross the field to it and along the church path.

St. Andrew's was once the parish church for the entire dale. Restored in the mid 19th century, only the tower base of this very large church remains from medieval times. Of many fine features inside, pride of place goes to the celebrated Jervaulx screen, a magnificent carved specimen rescued from the abbey at the Dissolution. Carvings in both wood and stone also feature in the beautiful pulpit and the reredos. To finish, turn down the path past the tower to find an enclosed way dropping down to Yore Mill, crossing the old mill cut on the way. Re-cross the bridge and take the path back up to the start.

14

CASTLE BOLTON

START Aysgarth   Grid ref. SE 011887

DISTANCE 7 miles

ORDNANCE SURVEY MAPS
1:50,000
Landranger 98 - Wensleydale & Upper Wharfedale
1:25,000
Outdoor Leisure 30 - Yorkshire Dales North/Central

ACCESS Start from the National Park car park at Aysgarth Falls, east of the village. Aysgarth is served by Leyburn-Hawes buses.

Easy walking visiting two of the valley's most famous features, one natural, one the work of man.

⑤ From the car park return to the road and turn left under the old railway bridge. A few yards after the station yard take a hand-gate on the right to enter a wood. A path rises through the trees, crossing a wide, green path to a hidden stile ahead, from where a string of gap-stiles point the way half-right through the fields. At the last stile turn left to a stile onto the farm road of Low Lane. Cross straight over it to pass through a long, narrow field, and from a stile on the right near the end, continue on to a gate between houses to emerge onto the road in Carperby, opposite the *Wheatsheaf Inn*.

Carperby is one of the most attractive and least spoilt villages in the dale. Its depth is virtually non-existant, for all its sturdy stone dwellings line the road running through the village. Standing well back from the valley bottom, it was once of greater importance as testified by the sizeable market cross. Dating from the seventeenth century it stands at one end of the narrow green. At the opposite end is a good grouping of chapels which have sadly been succumbing to modern trends: these include a Methodist chapel of 1820 and a Friends' Meeting House of 1864. It is said the Wensleydale breed of sheep was first named here.

Turn right a short distance and head up the first lane on the left. This 'no through road' rises out of the village to become a broad track between walls. Beyond a barn keep right at a fork to climb by the wall and round to a gate. A large tract of colourful, rough pasture is now entered, and with Bolton Castle in view down-dale, our near level approach to it can be well surveyed.

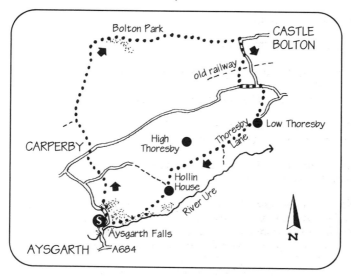

A generally clear green track heads on through the bracken to arrive at a gate at the far end, then crosses Beldon Beck and runs a little less clearly along to a gate in the right-hand wall. From here the track becomes wide and clear to lead through half a dozen more fields towards the imposing bulk of Bolton Castle. Through a narrow wood the track leads to the very walls of the castle.

Bolton Castle is a majestic ruin that cannot fail to impress the first time visitor. When approached from a distance it initially belies its ruinous condition. Originally a 14th century manor house, it was converted into a castle by Richard, the first Lord Scrope. Mary, Queen of Scots was a famous guest, being imprisoned here from 1568 to 1569. The castle and its improved facilities are open to visitors, its labyrinth of an interior being well worth exploring. Tearoom and gift shop are modern day essential additions. Though only the village has the 'Castle' prefixing the 'Bolton', the castle often gets the same treatment.

Although comprehensively overshadowed by its castle, the village of Castle Bolton is highly appealing in its own right. A spacious green separates two intermittent rows of cottages, many of which housed the lead miners of long ago. Today this is a peaceful place, which like Carperby is well up from the valley bottom. The church of St.Oswald stands almost at the castle wall. Dating back more than 600 years, this tiny place of worship reveals a surprisingly spacious interior.

— *Bolton Castle* —

Between castle and church we emerge onto the village street alongside the green, and from the corner it is this road we descend to leave Castle Bolton village. Soon a track forks right between barns, descending to two houses and the defunct railway line. Across the old line a charming, leafy snicket drops down to join a road. Go left along the road only as far as the Castle Bolton junction, then take a stile on the right. Cross to the far end of the field, and from the stile bear down right to another stile in the very bottom left corner. It leads to a small footbridge onto Thoresby Lane. Along to the right the lane quickly ends at Low Thoresby.

At a gate to the right of the farm the lane is born again, now as a delectable green byway. Centuries old, it feels little altered, and its snaking route between hedgerows is a joy throughout. **It finally terminates just beyond an extremely wet junction with Watery Lane.** That branch goes down to ford the Ure: be grateful we don't! **From a stile into a field follow the wall away to the next, then bear left over the brow to a stile near the far corner. Note that this section of old road is not currently marked on the OS map.**

A farm track is joined to lead down to Hollin House. Refreshments may be on offer here. The mighty wall of Penhill is a major feature of the lower dale, and from this vicinity it is in particularly dominant mood. **Advance into the farmyard, but then turn immediately down a track slanting away, and on to a gate into a large pasture. In the trees below is the turbulence of the Lower Falls, with Penhill immediately across the valley. Cross straight over to locate a stile ahead, from where a good path runs alongside a fence. Emerging from the trees, turn down to the left to join the terminus of the waterfalls path exactly at the Lower Falls.**

Aysgarth is made famous by its series of Upper, Middle and Lower Falls. Here the Yoredale series of limestone rocks make their greatest showing to create a water wonderland. It is the grand scale of things rather than their height that provides the spectacle. What makes all this truly beautiful is the setting - thickly wooded with rich plant life. **A distinctive gap in the cliffs permits a cul-de-sac descent to the water's-edge vantage point.**

Back at the stile a well trodden path heads up river, passing by a short, circular detour to a more intimate viewpoint for the Lower Falls. Up above, the path temporarily vacates the woodland before entering Freeholder's Wood to quickly reach the Middle Falls viewing platform. Freeholder's Wood was purchased by the National Park Authority to preserve its future, and coppicing of the woodland has been re-introduced. **Only yards further we emerge onto the road just below the car park entrance. To include the Upper Falls (best seen from Yore Bridge) turn down the road to gain the bridge, from where a path then leads directly back up to the car park.**

55

15

WALDEN VALLEY

START West Burton   Grid ref. SE 017866

DISTANCE 6½ miles

ORDNANCE SURVEY MAPS
1:50,000
Landranger 98 - Wensleydale & Upper Wharfedale
1:25,000
Outdoor Leisure 30 - Yorkshire Dales North/Central

ACCESS Start from the village centre. There is ample parking along-side the greens. Served by Leyburn-Aysgarth-Hawes buses.

An intimate exploration of an unfrequented side valley.

S The Walden Valley is one of the least known and least changed in the Dales, and the reason certainly for the former, is that it is a dead-end for motor vehicles. Not only that, the quiet lanes that set off up each side of the valley fail to connect again, thereby denying any circular tour. The individual farms are the only settlements up-dale of West Burton. The beck flows a good seven miles to reach the village, being born under the summit of Buckden Pike.

West Burton is an absolute gem of a village, not only well away from the main road through Wensleydale but also hidden from the lesser road that runs through Bishopdale to join it. Strictly speaking the village is in the Walden Valley, and jealously guards the only entrance to it. It features a pub, the *Fox & Hounds*, and a Post office/store. Outstanding is the extensive green, with cottages stood back in appreciation. An obelisk of 1820 stands on market cross steps, with village stocks nearby: 'round the back' are the delightful falls in a wooded dell. This is surely Wensleydale's best!

Depart the village green by a narrow lane on the left (ascending) signposted *Walden only*. When it forks take the left arm towards Walden South, and after a barn take a stile on the right. Here begins a long, largely pathless trek across the fields sloping down to Walden Beck. Mostly level, the ensuing amble requires little description: every intervening wall is graced with a stile.

The first deviation occurs after a good mile, when a wall deflects us half-right across a field with a beck in it. From the stile there cling to the perimeter of a fenced enclosure, beyond which a hand-gate precedes a footbridge over Cowstone Gill. Pass to the right of the house, over a stile, and head across the field to a gate opposite: through it a drive is joined to run along to Hargill Farm.

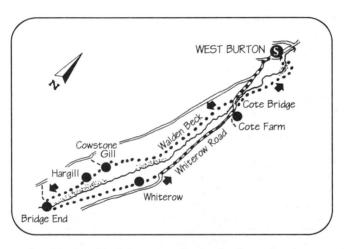

From the right-hand building cross the tiny beck to a hand-gate, and then resume a level march across the fields. Maintain this course through several more pastures before descending to the next farm, Bridge End. At this most distant point of the journey, take a stile a little beyond the buildings, then double back beneath them to a small farm bridge over Walden Beck. On the opposite bank go immediately through a stile on the left, and continue downstream to a stile in a fence. Now forsake the beck by climbing half-right to a gate at the top corner. From it turn left to commence a long, level march complementing that of the outward leg.

Once more virtually pathless, the only difference on this section is that gates have largely replaced stiles. Before long the farm of Whiterow appears ahead. Pass along the front of the buildings, from where its drive takes over to guide us out onto a lane. Turn left to follow its traffic-free course back down the valley, arriving at Cote Bridge over Walden Beck after a long mile. Just before reaching Cote Farm before the bridge, note the scant remains of a chimney that was part of the Burton Smelt Mill, serving lead mines in the late 17th and early 18th centuries.

Without crossing the bridge, take a gate on the right to accompany the beck downstream until reaching a footbridge over it. Once again forgo the crossing, and this time head half-right away from it to a stile. Rise up the side of the next field to a stile half-way, then break across the field to an easily located gap-stile. Now head straight across three further fields in a direct line: beyond this a track descends left, but we branch off it to a stile just before it reaches a gate.

Follow the left-hand wall around to reach the final stile, from where a path descends the edge of a field to a hand-gate on the left. Steps now lead down to a footbridge below West Burton Falls, which can be fully appreciated at closer range before turning right to emerge back into the village centre.

West Burton Falls

For more on West Burton see page 56.

16

COVERDALE MOORS

START West Burton   Grid ref. SE 018855

DISTANCE 11 miles

ORDNANCE SURVEY MAPS
1:50,000
Landranger 98 - Wensleydale & Upper Wharfedale
          99 - Northallerton & Ripon
1:25,000
Outdoor Leisure 30 - Yorkshire Dales North/Central

ACCESS Start from Cote Bridge, south of the village. There is reasonable parking just beyond the bridge, reached from the village centre by the road to 'Walden only'. Fork left at the first junction and the road descends to the bridge. Walking from West Burton adds an extra 1½ miles: there is better parking here, alongside the green. West Burton is served by Leyburn-Aysgarth-Hawes buses.

An invigorating if mildly strenuous walk, using two fine inter-valley paths on high moorland to visit two Coverdale villages. Not surprisingly the views are extensive: take your sandwiches and make a day of this one!

S For more on West Burton see page 56. **Leave Cote Bridge along the lane running past Cote Farm and up the valley, and remain on its traffic-free course for about 1¼ miles. Above a steep rise a guidepost indicates the departure of a bridle-road to Horsehouse. Take this track to the left, passing through a gate and rising to swing left to a gate onto the moortop. Now virtually level a good path heads away, but after only a short way be sure to opt for the lesser left branch at a fork. It crosses the undulating moor to another gate, becoming very clear again to reach the headwaters of the Fleensop valley.**

At another junction fork right to a gate, fording Fleemis Gill above a mini-ravine. This neighbourhood was the site of Fleensop Colliery, a modest sized coal mining operation. **The track now rises across Fleensop Moor, parallel with a nearby wall and passing grouse butts to reach a gate in the wall. The last section of moor is crossed more sketchily to join a wall on the right and follow it left.**

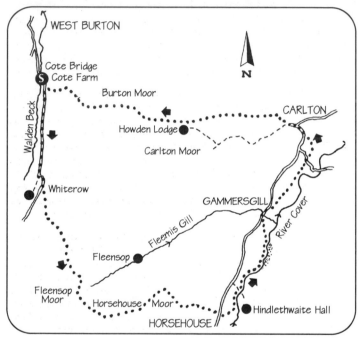

On this last stretch of moorland both Little and Great Whernsides appear at the head of Coverdale, which itself is unfolding increasingly rapidly ahead. **Use the first gate in the wall to begin the descent into Coverdale. Head down the pasture, ultimately bearing left to a stile in the bottom corner, and make use of the walled confines of a wooded beck to drop into Horsehouse.** This is the first sizeable community in the dale. Its pleasant grey buildings are arranged in a compact huddle, including a cosy little pub, the *Thwaite Arms*, and a modest church of 1869 dedicated to St. Botolph. On the road up-dale is a redundant Wesleyan chapel dated 1828.

Coverdale is longest of the Ure's side valleys. The road out of the valley leads over Park Rash to Kettlewell, and was part of the London to Richmond coaching route. A famous son of the dale was Miles Coverdale, who first translated the Bible into English. **Turn right only as far as the pub then take a lane running behind it for a short way to leave by a white gate down to the right. Descend to the next gate, left to another and then cross to a hand-gate right of a barn. The Cover is now joined and traced downstream for a mile. It is vacated at the end of the second enclosure after a pronounced wooded bend, crossing diagonally from the gate up to a red gate, and up again to a splendid stile well right of the buildings in view. A wooded enclosure leads onto the road in Gammersgill, an untouched farming hamlet.**

Go right along the road, soon leaving it by a gap-stile on the right. From it bear left to another stile to enter Turnbeck Lane, a narrow, green byway that is followed to its terminus. On emerging cross to a wall-corner and on again to the top far end of the next pasture. A beck is crossed to a well hidden stile in the top corner: continue across to accompany a fence, using a stile in it to reach a stile onto a narrow road. Head up as far as the next bend, then take a stile to cross a field bottom. From the next stile head for one in the top corner, then climb the field to a gate to emerge onto a road. Turn right for Carlton. For a note on the village please refer to page 78.

If not wishing to potter about the place, opt for a lane climbing left at the first junction at the edge of the village: here begins the second of the day's brace of moorland crossings. At once the lane starts to climb, and at a fork take the rough track going up to the right. It climbs steeply before rising across Carlton Moor, always with at least one wall for company. With the tree-shrouded Howden Lodge in view, the amenable track by-passes a short walled section before crossing an open pasture to approach the lodge's entrance.

Don't enter its confines but take the track climbing right. Gradients soon ease and the way continues through a collapsed wall before going right to a gate in the moortop wall. The track runs on to the brow of the hill on Burton Moor. Burton Moor is the southern edge of Penhill, and at 1591ft this summit of the walk makes a fitting spot for the final sojourn. The sudden view of the main valley is superb, with nearby Addlebrough featuring prominently. **Resuming, the track quickly launches itself into a rapid descent. In its latter, winding stages it becomes enclosed to emerge onto the road in the Walden Valley. Cote Bridge is just along to the right.** If you walked out from West Burton to Cote Bridge, WALK 15 offers a more attractive finish.

17

UNDER PENHILL

START West Burton   Grid ref. SE 017866

DISTANCE 7½ miles

ORDNANCE SURVEY MAPS
1:50,000
Landranger 98 - Wensleydale & Upper Wharfedale
1:25,000
Outdoor Leisure 30 - Yorkshire Dales North/Central

ACCESS Start from the village centre. There is ample parking along-side the greens. Served by Leyburn-Aysgarth-Hawes buses.

Exceptionally easy walking on Penhill's lower flanks, with West Witton village at the midway point. The return leg in particular affords superb Wensleydale views.

S For notes on West Burton please refer to WALK 15. **Follow the road back out of the village to the B6160. Go right a few yards with the beck then turn off over the arched Burton Bridge. Head along the narrow lane past Flanders Hall on the left, rising above Howraine Farm.** Our track is known as Morpeth Gate, a historic green road once used as a packhorse route. Already there are fine views ahead to Ivy Scar above Carperby and Bolton Castle: as the way improves, the distinctive flat-topped Addlebrough appears behind us.

During the second such rise look for a gate on the left *(Templars' Chapel 1 mile)* **and head along the field. Towards the end slant up to a gate at the end of the wall, then resume along the top of the clear wooded bank. This remains the route to reach a junction with a track rising from Temple Farm. Straight across we reach the Templars' Chapel.** The chapel of the Knights Templar is a little less exciting than it looks on the map. Here the low ruins of the chapel of the Penhill Preceptory include several stone graves (one illustrated on page 8), the structure itself dating from the early 13th century. Several adjoining buildings remained uncovered when this was excavated in 1840.

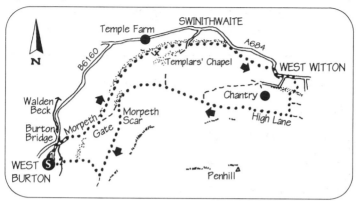

Resume as before along the field-side, interrupted only by crossing a firm track further on. A brief open section exploits the view over the dale: Castle Bolton, Redmire and Preston sit beneath their scars, with moorland above. **Reaching a stile onto the road, don't use it but bear right up to a stile in the wall ahead.** Penhill's dark wall rises steeply above. **Cross the brow to the far corner where a stile admits to the right edge of the small wood. Emerging at the other side advance to a gap-stile part-way on. From one in the corner behind cross to a stile onto the road at the edge of West Witton. Turn right into the village.**

West Witton is a pleasant village which suffers greatly by being split almost in two by the incessant traffic rumbling through. On the slopes of Penhill, it looks out across the valley from high above the river. The village boasts two pubs, the *Wensleydale Heifer* and the *Fox & Hounds*, and up until not that long ago even supported a third, the *Star*. West Witton is perhaps best known for an annual event here, the burning of Owd Bartle. An effigy, presumably of St. Bartholomew to whom the church is dedicated, is joyfully burnt in Guy Fawkes fashion. This occurs on the Saturday nearest his feast day in late August: its meaning seems to have gone up in the smoke of the years. The church itself is tucked secretively away down a back lane. Dating largely from Victorian times, it retains a 16th century tower.

Leave by the small garden on the right opposite the *Wensleydale Heifer*. By the little pond a snicket takes up between high walls to emerge into a field. Bear left to a gap-stile, then slant up to a gate and stile in the next hedge. Don't take it but turn up the field-side to the top corner. A stile admits to the trees and a path slants up the minor bank. At the top is a fork of paths. Go left a few yards to a stile, then continue away to join Watery Lane by its head. Cross straight over and along the field to a corner stile alongside a stream. Rise up by it to a stile onto High Lane. Turn right along the firm track of this old road. All is plain sailing for some time, indeed all the way back if so desired, for this is the continuation of Morpeth Gate.

At a junction with a similar lane from the right turn to look up at the quarried face of Penhill. The way resumes between broader verges and quickly reaches its high point. This is a fine moment as Wensleydale appears outspread in front (around this point a further branch joins from the right). Our lane drops down and runs on to a fork. A direct finish goes steeply down to the right, rejoining our outward route. The finest finish takes the track bearing left, rising above the bold Morpeth Scar just in front. From the edge is the first bird's-eye view of West Burton. The track soon becomes enclosed as Hudson Quarry Lane. At its demise a contrastingly faint green way takes over through rough pasture to quickly arrive at a wall-corner and guide-post. This is the emphatic turning point of the footpath. Up behind are the scars of old quarries. This is a superb viewpoint with West Burton itself seen in bird's-eye fashion below. Forelands Rigg divides the Walden Valley and Bishopdale.

A clear green path doubles back down to the right past a cairn, locating a gap-stile in the wall below. Immediately below is a steep and rough drop, with West Burton literally at our feet. Thankfully the path takes evasive action by invoking a good zigzag pattern to reach the stile directly below. From it a path runs left down a minor bank and bears left to the corner where a stile admits to the edge of Barrack Wood. It curves down the edge of the wood and at the first corner is another fork. A newly created link path crosses the stile on the left and descends the field to a crossroads of paths at a wall corner. Continue straight down, becoming enclosed at the corner from where a path descends the edge of a field to a hand-gate on the left. Steps now lead down to a footbridge below West Burton Falls, which can be fully appreciated at closer range (illustrated on page 58) before turning right to emerge back into the village centre.

```
┌─────────────────────────────────────┐
│              ⟨  18  ⟩                │
│                                      │
│      PENHILL BEACON                  │
│                                      │
└─────────────────────────────────────┘
```

START West Witton   Grid ref. SE 061883

DISTANCE 6 miles

ORDNANCE SURVEY MAPS
1:50,000
Landranger 98 - Wensleydale & Upper Wharfedale
*   99 - Northallerton & Ripon*
1:25,000
Outdoor Leisure 30 - Yorkshire Dales North/Central

ACCESS *Start from the village centre. There is scope for careful roadside parking only: ideally a large lay-by at the Leyburn end of the village is a more practical spot. West Witton is served by Leyburn-Aysgarth-Hawes buses.*

A grand climb to a fine viewpoint, using an absolutely superb selection of old tracks.

⑤   West Witton is a pleasant village which suffers greatly by being split almost in two by the incessant traffic rumbling through. On the slopes of Penhill, it looks out across the valley from high above the river. The village boasts two pubs, the *Wensleydale Heifer* and the *Fox & Hounds*, and up until not that long ago even supported a third, the *Star*.

West Witton is perhaps best known for an annual event here, the burning of Owd Bartle. An effigy, presumably of St. Bartholomew to whom the church is dedicated, is joyfully burnt in Guy Fawkes fashion. This occurs on the Saturday nearest his feast day in late August: its meaning seems to have gone up in the smoke of the years. The church itself is tucked secretively away down a back lane. Dating largely from Victorian times, it retains a 16th century tower.

65

Leave West Witton by a lane at the west (Aysgarth) end of the main street by a grassy triangle opposite the former school. Leaving the last of the dwellings behind it climbs to a crossroads of ways: go straight ahead and the lane becomes an enclosed track (Green Gate) to rise past an old quarry before arriving at a junction with a splendid green road known as High Lane. Take the gate in front and resume the rise on a green track, passing through two more gates before emerging onto a plateau directly beneath the cliffs of Penhill.

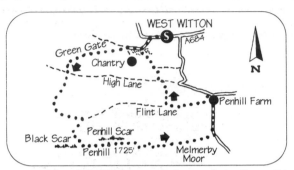

Our green path heads left before we fork away from the wall to cross to the most distant of four prominent spoil heaps. From it double back along the tops of the other three, exploring as you go. At the last of these a path (one of many) rises just behind, and gently scales an expertly engineered sunken way to the edge of Penhill's summit plateau, with Black Scar to the right and Penhill Scar to the left. This section from under the scar onto Melmerby Moor is not an official right of way, but stiles are provided at the only two obstacles, so if we behave there should be no problem. **Turn left along the wall to a stile, continuing on a sketchy path along the edge. The Ordnance column (S7708) is passed over the wall before arriving at a small cairn. Just a few yards further appears a mighty cairn on Penhill End.**

Penhill is Wensleydale's best known fell, its ability to stand out in views from afar greater than its popularity as a climb. When its top is gained, it is usually by a quick stroll from a car at the top of Melmerby Moor. Its abrupt edge renders Penhill identifiable from most parts of Wensleydale, and is a regular feature of views west from the North York Moors. Penhill's own virtues as a viewpoint are assisted by the dramatic plunge of the scar, the top of which provides bird's-eye pictures of the lower dale. It is the afore-mentioned advantages which have given the hill historical significance. It was the site of a beacon, one of a chain throughout the land which when lit could rapidly spread the message of some impending danger such as the Spanish Armada. Less certain is the idea that this is an Iron age chieftain's last resting place.

Strictly speaking, the true summit of Penhill is a mile to the south-west of the Ordnance Survey column, but an hour's return plod is not recommended. To clarify what exactly is what on the summit plateau, the true top is over 1800ft, the OS column is at 1725ft, and the small cairn on the mound (the beacon site) is 1685ft. To the east, and a little lower still, is the big cairn on Penhill End.

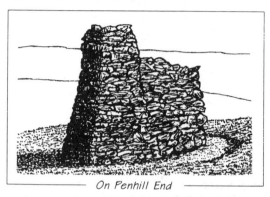
On Penhill End

Our descent over Melmerby Moor is well laid out below, as is an alternative bridleway through fields to the left. A path drops directly from the cairn to a stile in the wall corner below, though various trods bypass the steepness and thereby protect the vulnerable terrain. From the stile a good path remains close to the wall to cross the moor to the crest of the Melmerby-West Witton road.

Go left over the cattle-grid and down to Penhill Farm, after which turn left along an enclosed track, Flint Lane. Tread its level course as far as a stile a short distance beyond a clump of trees, from where a steep field is descended to a stile onto a similar green lane (High Lane again). From the stile opposite descend two further fields onto a third and final green lane. Go left to a barn then bear right across the field behind to a stile. Peer over the fence ahead to see a waterfall in the wood, then take a wicket-gate to the left. A path crosses the caravan site at Chantry to leave by a similar gate, then descends steeply through trees onto the lane by which we departed the village.

19

REDMIRE FORCE

START *West Witton*   *Grid ref. SE 061883*

DISTANCE *6¾ miles*

ORDNANCE SURVEY MAPS
1:50,000
Landranger 98 - Wensleydale & Upper Wharfedale
*   99 - Northallerton & Ripon*
1:25,000
Outdoor Leisure 30 - Yorkshire Dales North/Central

ACCESS *Start from the village centre. Careful roadside parking only: there is a large lay-by at the Leyburn end of the village. West Witton is served by Leyburn-Aysgarth-Hawes buses.*

Easy walking and easy route finding. Included is the best long section of riverbank in the valley.

S For notes on West Witton please refer to page 65. **At the east (Leyburn) end of the village take a walled track just after the last house on the left. Almost at once it forks, and here take the right-hand option, known as Back Lane.** On descending note the stately Bolton Hall on the opposite bank. Set in graceful parkland, this was the home of the Lords Bolton dating back three centuries. WALK 20 gets a close-up view of it.

Twisting and turning, the way leads steadily downhill towards the river, narrowing in its later stages. At its demise do not use the gate directly in front, but opt for the gap-stile by a gate on the right. Entering the field adhere to the left-hand boundary wall until its various indentations lead down to a gateway with the Ure now in close proximity.

Cross the stream behind and drop to a stile in the fence to the right to gain the riverbank. Plain sailing now ensues as the Ure is traced updale through a succession of quiet pastures. Despite being a major valley, Wensleydale only attracts large numbers to its river at a very short stretch at Aysgarth. This much less-known section however provides outstanding company for several beautifully wooded miles.

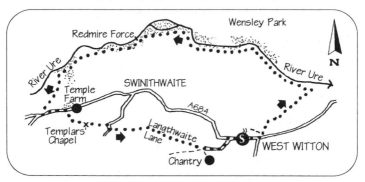

Eventually, beyond a large, wooded island and a lively bend, a wall commences to separate us from the river. Stay with the wall through a couple of fields, at the end of which a stile admits to the thickly wooded bank. A path runs through the trees, and almost immediately Redmire Force greets the eye. The splendour of this scene is the scale of the Aysgarth-like falls on this wide section of river, not to mention the wooded surrounds and general lack of fellow humans!

No sooner has the path deposited us alongside the falls then it is away again, forsaking the river by climbing a stairway to a stile out of the woods. A generally straight line now ensues through a succession of fields, all served by stiles. High above the wooded riverbank the route follows a fence to two neighbouring stiles, from where the fence heads across an extensive pasture. When it bends away, continue on ahead to a stile in the far corner.

A good path drops down through trees to briefly rejoin the river, but on emerging into a large riverside pasture we leave it for the last time. Following the wall curving away up to the left, a partially enclosed track materialises to lead onto the main road. Almost opposite note a boundary post (Aysgarth/Leyburn) and also an inscribed stone similar to the one illustrated overleaf, to be seen by the gate above the chapel.

Being wary of the traffic, turn left up the hill to a stile on the right just short of Temple Farm. In the trees opposite is a roadside curiosity, built in 1792 as a belvedere (viewing platform) by the owners of nearby Swinithwaite Hall. **From the stile follow a farm track running to the top end of the field. It enters a belt of woodland, and on emerging at the top a stile on the left gives access to the remains of the Knights Templars' Chapel.**

The chapel of the Knights Templar is a little less exciting than it looks on the map. Here the low ruins of the chapel of the Penhill Preceptory include several graves, the structure itself dating from the early 13th century. Several adjoining buildings remained uncovered when this was excavated in 1840. **From the chapel a sketchy track rises to the top of the field, going on to join a concrete farm road.**

Follow the farm road uphill only as far as a bend right, then bear left up a vague track to the top of the field. Here Penhill appears directly above, looking moody and menacing in the right conditions. **From a gap-stile in the angle of the wall head across a level pasture to a gateway, and with a wall on the right, follow it along to the terminus of a green lane. This is Langthwaite Lane, and all is now very much plain sailing as this superb way is trodden all the way back to West Witton. Towards the end it meets a narrow road to descend into the village.**

*Above:
an inscribed
stone near
the chapel*

The Wensleydale Heifer, West Witton

20

BOLTON HALL

START Redmire   Grid ref. SE 046912

DISTANCE 5½ miles

ORDNANCE SURVEY MAPS
1:50,000
Landranger 98 - Wensleydale & Upper Wharfedale
          99 - Northallerton & Ripon
1:25,000
Outdoor Leisure 30 - Yorkshire Dales North/Central

ACCESS Start from the village centre. Reasonable parking around (but not on!) the village green. Served by Leyburn-Hawes buses.

Very easy walking through the lush pastures of the lower dale.

S   Redmire sits just outside the National Park, but its attractive green and attendant houses are equal to many within. Sat upon the green is a pillar erected to celebrate Victoria's Golden Jubilee in 1887. The village surprisingly boasts two pubs, the *Bolton Arms* and *Kings Arms*, and also a Post office/store.

From the green turn down the main road in the Carperby direction (up-dale). At a sharp bend right, go straight ahead on Church Lane. At an immediate fork go left for a few minutes' stroll along this cul-de-sac to the church. St. Mary the Virgin's is a delightful little church hidden away in peaceful seclusion. Dating from the 12th century it features a splendid carved Norman doorway and a simple bell-cote. The churchyard is a riot of snowdrops at the back end of winter.

Back on the lane, return just as far as the overflow car park and take a narrow gap-stile on the left. Double back left across the field to another stile onto Well Lane, a hedgerowed way. Go left to the

second sharp bend, and as the green lane goes right, advance straight on through a gate/stile into the field. Head away with a stream to the far end, and from the slab and stile there the way is clearly marked by successive stiles as it approaches West Wood in the Bolton Hall grounds. In the last field a faint green way slant up to a tall iron kissing-gate into the trees.

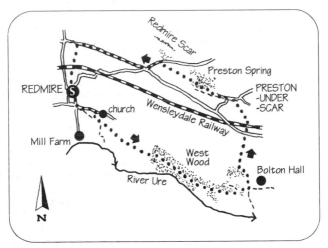

Just ahead is a junction of carriageways. Go straight ahead on the one forging into the trees. Within minutes we are treated to superb vistas over the Ure far below, with Penhill glimpsed high above West Witton. After one or two open sections on the right we emerge to run on to a junction with a firmer drive and Bolton Hall itself just ahead. Though our way turns up to the left, advance for a minute along the drive to appraise the lovely frontage. Bolton Hall was for three centuries the seat of the once influential Scrope family, the Lords Bolton. Note the iron gates 'B 1930' referring to the Lords Bolton.

Back at the junction turn up the firm track which rises past the farm buildings, bearing left at the top and then continuing to rise up to meet a road opposite the house at Stoneham. Cross straight over and up some steps to a gate into a field, with Preston-under-Scar outspread just ahead. Cross to the left of a barn where the railway line is met in a minor cutting. For more on the Wensleydale Railway see page 76. Across, bear gently left up the field to a gap-stile left of a storage building. Bear left again up the field to locate a gap-stile

in front of modern houses at the topmost corner. A snicket rises up onto a drive and thence the road. Go left along the street, keeping straight on when the through road turns down to the left. Preston is an unassuming place, with a tiny triangle green and an old tap watched over by St. Margaret's church, almost lost in a row of houses. Hidden up to the right is a hall dedicated to the six parishioners who fell in the first world war. At the end of the street is a tiny village store.

At the end of the street a drive takes over, and beyond a few houses take the branch right. This is left at once by a hand-gate to its left, and a path runs across mixed ground in front of a lone house. At the end the woods of Preston Spring are entered and a good path runs on through the trees. Ahead is a first glimpse of stately Bolton Castle. **Emerging, keep on in grand surrounds to a stile onto a road at the far end.** High up to the right is the gleaming limestone of the long, unbroken line of Redmire Scar.

Note a track opposite running to a gate into the field ahead and shown on the map by a pecked line: it is a good example of a 'lost' path, for though not recorded as a public right of way on the definitive map, it is clearly a historic route. It runs on for three-quarters of a mile to rejoin our route above Redmire. Further along it are sunken and part-hedgerowed enclosed sections, while sturdy gap-stiles are still in place, if largely blocked up, alongside gates. Perhaps one day it will be restored to public use to save our (albeit very peaceful) road walk.

Please, therefore, remain with me and descend to the road junction just down the hill. Go right here, and keep right along an almost hidden narrow byway as the main road drops into Redmire. This traffic-free course ais punctuated by one or two gates and has a grassy central strip. You can enjoy stunning views over to Penhill, Bishopdale, over Redmire and ahead to Castle Bolton.

On becoming fully unenclosed a footpath is crossed: keep straight on to the next footpath sign. Here turn down to the left alongside a hedge. At the bottom of the bank is a gap-stile. Head down the field, and in the next one keep right of farm buildings to find a gap-stile into undergrowth. Just below it crosses straight over a track and reaches the railway line and sidings. Redmire's station is just along to the left: in 2004 this re-opened as the present terminus of the Wensleydale Railway. **Cross and continue down to the bottom corner of the next field, then down with a stream to a gap-stile into the edge of the village. Head down the drive to emerge back onto the green.**

21

LEYBURN SHAWL

START Leyburn   Grid ref. SE 112904

DISTANCE 5½ miles

ORDNANCE SURVEY MAPS
1:50,000
Landranger 99 - Northallerton & Ripon
1:25,000
Outdoor Leisure 30 - Yorkshire Dales North/Central

ACCESS Start from the market square in the centre. Ample car parking. Served by bus from Masham, Richmond and Hawes.

A very easy walk with a variety of interest: the renowned Shawl is worth the walk itself, but beyond it are old lead workings, the parkland of Bolton Hall and the charming village of Wensley.

S The busy little town of Leyburn is the true gateway to Wensleydale. Focal point is a vast market place which still serves its original function on Fridays, when dalesfolk from miles around add further colour to the scene. At the top stands the imposing town hall of 1856, while several pubs and cafes do brisk trade. Just off the market place are found 18th century Leyburn Hall; Thornborough Hall, enlarged to its present state in 1863; St. Matthew's church of 1868 (features furnishings from the famous 'Mouseman' workshops of Kilburn); and the relatively early Roman Catholic church of St. Peter & St. Paul, dating back to 1835. The town has a Tourist Information Centre and is also home to the Wensleydale Show, which occurs in late August.

Leave the market place by the old town hall, crossing the top road to Commercial Square, with the *Bolton Arms* on the left. At the top of the small square, quaint *'Way to the Shawl'* signs point up a side street, turning left at the top to a kissing-gate into a field corner. Head away along the forming grassy edge, the start of the Shawl.

Leyburn Shawl was laid out as a place of promenade in 1841, a typical Victorian Sunday afternoon attraction. The Queen's Gap, further along but not easy to determine, is so named as Mary, Queen of Scots was allegedly recaptured here after brief freedom from Bolton Castle. This initial stretch is popular with dog walkers, while there are seats galore from which to appraise the view of Penhill across the dale.

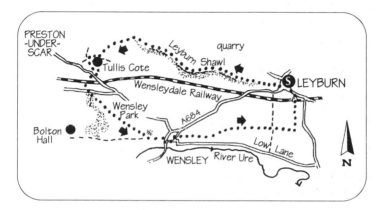

Advance along the edge, modest limestone outcrops appearing as the path runs on above the woods. This continues for a while through several stiles before the path passes through a stile to enter the top of the woods. The finest, long section now begins, enjoying panoramic views over the dale. The path forges on and the situation constantly improves, with a sheer scar beneath our feet: young 'uns take care. The presence of a vast quarry over to the right is largely immaterial thanks to a high wall.

Eventually the trees, and with them the Shawl end. The path drops down a little to a stile, then slants down to a crumbling wall and the very last few trees. Head down the field to a stile by a gate at the bottom, then slant across to the next one. Head along the field bottom through outcrops and banks of an ancient settlement and field system. A track forms to turn down through a gate in the wall below, and runs down to a junction. Bear right to Tullis Cote Farm. At the crossroads of tracks at the end of the buildings note the fine four-arched building ahead and the mighty spring emerging just in front. Don't cross, but turn sharp left down the outside of the farm buildings, absorbing the drive to descend onto a back road.

75

En route we pass the site of a smelt mill from an old lead mine, the old buildings still very evident despite dense undergrowth. Most prominent however is the tall, square chimney. At the road first look along to the right to see the beautifully converted Preston Mill, a three-storey house. **Cross to the gate opposite and across to the railway line.**

The Wensleydale Railway was a 40 mile link between the Vale of York and the Pennines. The line reached Hawes in 1878 and on to Garsdale Head (then Hawes Junction) where it linked with the Settle-Carlisle line. The last passenger service ran in 1954 and the rails removed above Redmire in 1965. The lower 22 miles remained to serve a limestone quarry on the moor edge above Redmire, but in 1992 this traffic ceased and the line became redundant save for an occasional military train bringing armoured vehicles towards Catterick Garrison. A campaign to save the line has made remarkable progress, with scheduled passenger services re-starting in 2003 from Leeming Bar as far as Leyburn, and extended to Redmire just a year later. There remains a long-term aim of re-instating the missing 18 miles, and who would bet against it? Just along to the left is the old station. **Cross the field behind to a gate onto another road.**

Go left for a couple of minutes then turn down a cart track into woods on the right. Almost at once a guidepost directs us left on a thinner path to a gate out of the trees. Cross the field, keeping above the wood top to a gap in the sharply angled fence ahead. Here enter the vast expanse of Wensley Park, in the grounds of Bolton Hall. The extensive view ahead features Middleham far down-dale, while the immediate foreground might reveal wild deer running for cover. **The invisible path slants down above a couple of old buildings on the right then gradually down the park, ultimately gaining the main drive at a gate just short of trees in the far corner. Go left to immediately join the road in Wensley.**

Wensley is a delightfully attractive village, largely out of character with the typical Dales villages upstream. This is in part due to the fact that this once important market town that gave its name to the valley was decimated by the Plague in 1563, and never recovered its status. A market charter was granted in 1202. Pride of place goes to the Holy Trinity church, dating from 1240. It contains various memorials to the Scropes, including their late 17th century family pew, and also an early 16th century rood screen. The graceful bridge dates back to the 15th century, though obviously much enlarged in the intervening years. Village pub is the *Three Horseshoes*, while visitors are also welcome at a candlemakers in the old mill. Our route enters the village at a tiny green featuring a water pump.

Across the road turn down to the right and quickly left along the Middleham road (Low Lane) above the church. Immediately over a bridge turn left up a narrow back lane. At the second bend, where it turns sharp left, leave by a gate on the right. Cross to a stile then on a longer field bottom. At the end stile slant up to one at the top of the wood in front and head away again. Part-way on a stile sees us to the other side. This is Old Glebe Field, a nature reserve of the Yorkshire Wildlife Trust. **Rise over a tiny stream to a stile in the top corner. The way is now obvious as a lengthy but pleasant trek ensues through the fields, pretty much a direct line and marked by a rich variety of stiles. Ultimately the way runs on to discover Low Wood Lane in a wooded hollow.**

Cross straight over and resume on a pleasant bank. Middleham is now much clearer to the right, while above us the edge of Leyburn awaits. **The stile at the end takes on the opposite side of the wall to the map, but from the waiting gap-stile at the end bear up to the left. A stile at the top has Leyburn church tower waiting prominently above. Continue up to find new housing intruding on the line of the path. Joining a little cul-de-sac go right half a dozen yards to find the path preserved, an enclosed way climbing between the houses to a drive. Go up again to join a road bridge over the railway line and up onto the main road near the bottom end of the market place.**

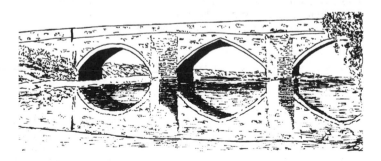

Wensley Bridge

22

COVERDALE

START *Carlton* *Grid ref. SE 068847*

DISTANCE *4½ miles*

ORDNANCE SURVEY MAPS
1:50,000
Landranger 99 - Northallerton & Ripon
1:25,000
Outdoor Leisure 30 - Yorkshire Dales North/Central

ACCESS *Start from the village centre. Various parking along the main street between the village hall and the pub without blocking access.*

S Carlton-in-Coverdale (Sunday name) is one of many linear villages in the district, and here the string of attractive buildings seems almost endless. The village features a pub, the *Foresters Arms*, the tiny church of Christ the Good Shepherd, and a Wesleyan Methodist chapel of 1873 in a lovely stream-side setting. A grassy knoll behind the pub is the site of a castle of which little is known. On the north side of the street at Flatts Farm is a large tablet inscribed *Henry Constantine of Carlton the Coverdale Bard, Feb 14th 1861.*

From the vicinity of the village hall head up the main street past the pub. Shortly after, a footpath is sent left along a drive. Continue up however, to the Methodist chapel, with Flatts Farm just a little further on. Back at the bridge outside the chapel, turn down an enclosed footway that runs by a tiny beck round the back of the houses. As it broadens into a drive (the earlier footpath branch) take a gap-stile on the right.

Here we are immediately out in the open, with a long wall of moorland stretching across the other side of the valley, leading up towards the Whernsides. **Double back across the field to the next** stile, continuing through a handful of first-rate gap-stiles to emerge onto a road corner. **Without treading tarmac take a gate on the left and descend to a prominent gap-stile at the bottom.** Just across the valley note some superb examples of strip lynchets (early farmers' cultivation terraces). **Bear right from this to a wall-corner stile, then on the field-side to join Cover Lane.**

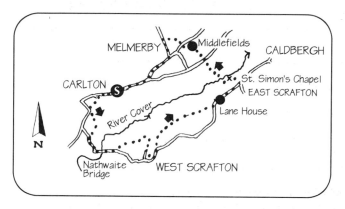

Turn down this narrow road to Nathwaite Bridge, a fine arched structure over the river Cover. Just two minutes up the other side, take a signposted gate on the left *(footpath to West Scrafton)* and immediately pass through another gate behind it. Now slant across the field to a stile at the bottom of a short section of wall opposite. Looking back now there is a fine prospect of Penhill ranged across the skyline high above straggling Carlton. **Head away briefly as far as a gate in the fence, then slant up the field to a fence-stile visible near the top.** Visible now are the edges of those lynchets that were seen a little earlier. **The quickest way into West Scrafton is up through the line of trees to a kissing-gate above, which then gives direct access to the village.**

More interestingly don't use the gate but turn left along the field top. At the end is a ladder-stile, from where turn up outside the wooded confines of Caygill. Just a little higher there are good glimpses into the deep craggy ravine of Caygill Scar. Just yards further it abates entirely, and a farm bridge crosses it. To omit West Scrafton, go over the bridge and across to a stile at the other side of the field to join Low Lane. **As the village well merits a visit, stay on this side of the stream** to rise up to a green and a drive on the edge of the village. A little further, a stream-side path branches off the green to rise to the village 'centre'.

West Scrafton is well off the beaten track and looks more than happy to remain so. The little green where the village path emerges is a delightful focal point. This tiniest of greens sits amongst some attractive houses, including the Manor House and the little Methodist Chapel built as a Primitive Methodist Chapel in 1866. Seat, phone box, Victorian postbox and a little tap all add their contribution, while a house set back from the earlier green bears a 1689 datestone. The bridge, meanwhile, sits astride a dark ravine, while just across it the fellside falls all the way to the village as tracks head off over the moors to both Colsterdale and Nidderdale.

St. Simon's Chapel

Crossing the bridge head out of the village and at the village sign bear left off the road down an enclosed track, Low Lane. At a fork the direct path from Caygill comes in at a stile. Here bear up to the right, the lane soon improving into a fine green way. At its demise keep straight on the field-side, and at the end cross to a gate ahead. Now bear right to find a stile in the tiniest section of wall in the corner, then sharp right to a similar arrangement alongside a tiny stream.

Cross the stream and contour left across the field to the deeper, wooded Thorow Gill, where a wooden footbridge is found to ease the crossing. Note the original fallen old slab below. Up the other side cross the field to a stile onto a lane. **Go left for just a few minutes as far as a minor junction with the access road into the hamlet of East Scrafton.** Across the valley Penhill End rises prominently above Melmerby. **On the left a stile sends us down the field-side to the wooded banks of the Cover. A part-stepped old path slants down to the riverbank.**

Here stands a big old limekiln on the left, while on the right the site of an ancient ford is still evident as an old hollowed lane, now unusable, drops down to the river. Main feature however is the forlorn yet atmospheric ruin of St. Simon's Chapel by the river. It was actually dedicated to St. Simon & St. Jude, and is thought to be over 600 years old. Immediately upstream is a lively spring which exists for literally a few yards before joining the river. This is St. Simon's Well, a holy well of great antiquity itself, and no doubt once treated with great reverence in its own right.

Turn upstream a short way past the well to St. Simon's Bridge (a modern footbridge) on the river in a grand little corner. On the other side go right a few yards to find a modern stepped path doubling back up through Scar Wood. At the top rise left up the field to a gap-stile, and continue directly up two fields to emerge onto a road. A direct finish goes left, but otherwise go right several yards to a gate, and head up the field to the barns of Middlefields Farm. At a stile onto the track turn left on it in front of the buildings and rises up onto the higher lane.

Again one could go left to finish, but otherwise advance just several yards to a gate and rise up the narrow enclosure. At the top rise left from the wall to meet a firmer track, then left towards Manor Farm. Approaching a traditional old barn (keep above all buildings) don't enter the yard but take a gateway to its right, and cross the enclosure via a wooden footbridge to a stile onto the lane at the head of Melmerby.

Turn left down the street to a T-junction. Melmerby is a peaceful farming settlement on Penhill's lower slopes. Down the street we pass a phone box and the humble Methodist chapel of 1893 furtively tucked round the back of a house. At the road junction stands an old milestone. **Go right along the lane to another junction, then right again to quickly re-enter straggling Carlton.**

23

MIDDLEHAM LOW MOOR

START *Coverham*   *Grid ref. SE 102863*

DISTANCE *6½ miles*

ORDNANCE SURVEY MAPS
1:50,000
Landranger 99 - Northallerton & Ripon
1:25,000
Outdoor Leisure 30 - Yorkshire Dales North/Central

ACCESS *Start from the junction in front of the church. Parking here or down the lane just before the bridge.*

This leisurely ramble takes in several of lower Coverdale's interesting features.

S   Coverham enjoys a sylvan setting at the lower end of its dale, well and truly off the normal tourist routes. Though barely even a hamlet it boasts a great deal of interest. The abbey was founded by Premonstratensian canons, and the scant remains include 14th century arches by a private house. Also largely defunct now is the church of the Holy Trinity, though the old bridge, at least, still serves its purpose.

Leave Coverham by crossing the bridge over the Cover and taking the quiet back road to Caldbergh. Turn up into the village on a lane that terminates at the last of the houses. Caldbergh is one of a number of tiny settlements in this neighbourhood which remain pleasantly unspoilt. **At a gate a farm track takes up the running, and is followed along to the left over several cattle-grids to arrive at Ashes Farm. A track then continues across the fields to cease at the second gate reached.**

Continue with a wall on the left, and at the next gate this too calls it a day. Head straight across to a gate in a fence, then cross an extensive pasture by passing a plantation. Here we have good views of Coverham Abbey and, well above it, Middleham Low Moor. Gradually declining to the far corner, a stile by a gate admits onto a road. Turn right on it, past a farm and along to the drive of Braithwaite Hall, with the familiar National Trust sign in evidence. Dated 1667, Braithwaite Hall is a splendid three gabled house in the care of the Trust, and though still in use as a farm it can be visited by prior arrangement.

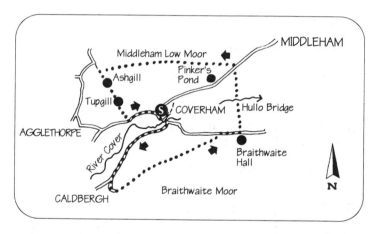

Opposite the drive is a gate, from where a track heads away on a steady descent to the river. The Cover is crossed by the stone arched Hullo Bridge. By far the longest of the Ure's tributaries in the Dales, the river Cover is a wonderfully unspoilt stream flowing from the flanks of Buckden Pike and Great Whernside to merge into the main river beneath Cover Bridge (see WALK 25). From the bridge a track bears left up the steep bank, an early right fork being the key to a sketchy, direct climb up a large pasture. At the top a gate precedes the unfenced Coverham-Middleham road over Middleham Low Moor.

Head straight up the opposite slope to join a wide track which can be followed left to a wall corner. It can be rewarding to divert a little left off the track to enjoy a bird's-eye view over the whole of Pinker's Pond. Attractive Pinker's Pond is on the site of an old quarry but often dry these days. **From the wall corner the track can be abandoned by striking a little to the right across the largely pathless moor. This couldn't be much less like the moors to which we are accustomed, and the short-cropped turf is a joy to feel underfoot. While keeping an eye open for racehorses the Ordnance column (S7586) at 760ft soon appears ahead, and is quickly attained.**

Middleham is rightly renowned for its horse-racing connections and the moor is a favourite venue for putting the horses through their paces. On our crossing of it, note the fine view of two valleys (Cover left and Ure right) divided by Penhill.

Gateway arch, Coverham Abbey

From the trig. point continue along the moortop's broad crest a good while yet: the boundary wall on the left remains in view for the most part, and on seeing the first set of buildings behind it head in that direction. Do not leave the moor here but accompany a wall-side track, and within a couple of minutes a solid drive is met. This heads through a gate and down to the left, passing between the buildings of Ashgill Stables and alongside the stables of Tupgill to drop down the drive onto the road.

Turn left along the road, passing the sad shell of a creamery of recent demise and soon arriving at the junction at Coverham church. The right branch leads straight back down to the bridge, but a visit to the church can be incorporated by the lych-gate just ahead. A path also leads from its right (south) side down onto the lane to Coverham Abbey, which itself merits a look to conclude the journey in fitting manner.

24

COVER BANKS

START *Middleham*   *Grid ref. SE 127877*

DISTANCE *5½ miles*

ORDNANCE SURVEY MAPS
1:50,000
Landranger 99 - Northallerton & Ripon
1:25,000
Outdoor Leisure 30 - Yorkshire Dales North/Central
Explorer 302 - Northallerton & Thirsk

ACCESS *Start from the town centre. Ample parking in the square and also higher up at the top end. Served by Ripon-Leyburn buses.*

Very easy walking based on the beautifully wooded lowest reach of the river Cover, with attractive bridges and old pubs in between.

S Middleham is an absorbing town; a village in size perhaps, but unquestionably a town in stature. It is famous for both its horse-racing connections (there are numerous stables in the area) and its castle, and is the historic gateway to Wensleydale. The castle ruins dominate, finest features being the massive Norman keep and the 14th century gatehouse. The castle was for centuries the stronghold of the powerful Neville family: known as the 'Windsor of the North', its best known Neville occupant was Richard, Earl of Warwick, 'the King-maker'. His daughter married Richard, Duke of Gloucester, who came to live here, later of course to become, briefly, the much maligned Richard III. His son Edward was born here, becoming Prince of Wales. The castle is owned by English Heritage (admission fee).

A cross at the head of the town recalls the grant obtained in 1479 for a twice yearly fair and market by Richard, when Duke of Gloucester: the carved stone is possibly a white boar, which was his badge.

85

Alongside are a Jubilee Fountain; the old school of 1869, now an interesting shop with crafts featuring sculpture; and a fine sundial dated 1778 on a house. The parish church of St. Mary & St. Alkelda goes back in part to the 14th century, and includes a monument from about 1533 to Abbott Robert Thornton of Jervaulx. The 14th century font boasts a striking 10ft high cover. Adjacent are the dignified three bays of Kingsley House, the former rectory dating from 1752.

Centrepiece of modern day social life is the small sloping square, surrounded by a healthy number of pubs and tearooms. Another market cross stands here on ancient tiered steps, and on summer Sundays a market still takes place. Each day though, one can witness elegant and valuable horses being lead up onto the moor to exercise on the gallops. Considering the rich appeal, in every aspect, of the place, tourism has barely taken hold, and the little town maintains a genuine atmosphere of its own.

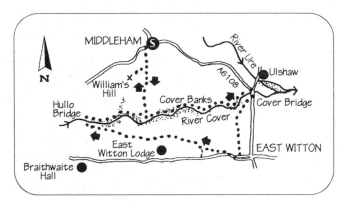

Leave the main street by going to the castle. Pass to its left and along an enclosed track outside the castle walls. At the end it emerges into a field with several options. Simply head up the wall-side, over the brow and down to the corner. Two stiles in quick succession gain the next field, then head down the wall-side past a barn. Ahead, the deeply enclosed environs of the river Cover await, with Braithwaite Moor and then Penhill further along to the right. **Pathless, the way descends all the way to the very riverbank.** Becoming more wooded at the bottom, this is a fine moment as the river rolls beneath the dark walls of Cover Scar.

Take a stile on the left and head downstream. A small path soon enters woodland, and then climbs above the river before dropping back down to leave the wood. Continue on a short way, and instead of being deflected left up a green track, remain on the riverbank to find a good path reforming to run hard by the rocky bank. This emerges again and runs on to some stepping stones. A dozen massive blocks form a foolproof crossing other than in spate, and it seems criminal not to be using them as a short-cut to East Witton!

Resuming down our bank, take a stile in front and then soon after, ignore another green track rising to the left: instead, take a stile into the sliver of woodland along the riverbank. The way is now clear and most enjoyable as the path clings to the river to reach the pub at Cover Bridge (unlike the map, the path does cling to the river here). At the buildings we are deflected left to a gap-stile onto the road. Just along to the left are Ulshaw Bridge and church (see WALK 25). Here at Cover Bridge, meanwhile, the homely *Coverbridge Inn* perches on the riverbank. If wanting an extended walk, WALK 25 could be added on at this point, the return to Cover Bridge taking probably 3 hours.

Cross the bridge and take some steps on the right down to the riverbank. Cross a stile onto the very bank opposite the pub garden, but instead of following the Cover upstream, stay with the hedge as it curves round to the left. Go on to a stile/gate near the end, then resume along the hedge through two further stiles. Here a guidepost sends a path right towards the stepping stones, but our way heads directly on, through a gate in a fence and on to a stile by a tiny barn. Pass round the back to a gap-stile then go left with the wall. Maintain this line until on a minor brow East Witton appears ahead. In a smaller enclosure take a small gate on the left at the end of the hedge, and head along the last field to emerge into the village street.

East Witton suffered terribly at the hands of the Plague in 1563, and was rebuilt as an estate village by the Earl of Ailesbury at the beginning of the 19th century. The church stands just east of the village, built in 1809 and dedicated to St. John the Evangelist. The two lines of houses are set back from a vast, sweeping green, which features a quoits pitch and an old waterpump. There is a Wesleyan Methodist chapel of 1882 at the point we entered the village, and a Post Office/store. At the main road corner is the attractive former school. Opposite is the *Blue Lion* pub, open for business again after a closed spell. On this corner also is a working tap embedded in a boulder.

Leave by turning right along the street, and at the end of the green a narrow road heads out of the village. Almost at once take a stile by a gate on the right. Two invisible paths head away: one goes to the stepping stones (again!), while ours bears left to a gap-stile at the far end. Continue with the hedge on the right through two further fields to join grassy West Field Lane. Turn right along this leafy pathway to its demise at a small wood. Though the map shows the path passing along its left side, it is in fact waymarked (and only passable) along its far side. At the end of the track don't take the gate into the field, but go left on a pleasant path running on to the far end of the trees.

Emerging into a field, go left and continue on to find a farm track forming. When it turns left through a gateway to approach the farm at East Witton Lodge, leave it and stay on another wall-side track. Through the gate at the end remain with the hedge on the right. When this kinks, slant across to rejoin it and remain with it past a small building to pass through a gate in the hedge. On the other side continue on to the very corner.

Here a footbridge crosses a tiny stream to emerge into a big pasture. Cross straight over the centre, a marker post on the brow assisting. Cross to the far right corner, dropping down to a gap-stile 50 yards to the left. Drop down to a step-stile below then head left along the fence-side, atop a wooded brow overlooking the river Cover. Towards the end drop down to reach Hullo Bridge. There is some splendid river scenery here as the Cover runs through a modest ravine and over a slabby limestone bed.

Across, take a stile on the right and head downstream. Almost at once the path climbs the wooded bank into a field. Resume along the top of the bank, all the way on to rise to a slim plantation. Twin stiles send a ten-yard path through it to resume along the wood top. As it starts to drop back down to the river, take advantage of the fact that the true course of the footpath contours left, perfect for us as we work round to meet the wall-cum-fence opposite. Now back on the outward route, turn up with it to be back in Middleham within minutes.

The brow has glorious views over the lower valley. On re-entering the head of the lane back to the castle, a detour can be made by taking the gap-stile on the left. From it slant up the field to a gate in the fence, then continue up to inspect the prominent William's Hill. This wooded knoll is the site of a 'ring and bailey', where a timber castle long preceded the main attraction below. It consists of an outer bank, ditch and inner bank. Concealed within is a small level centrepiece, where a 40ft high motte stood. Certainly its siting was unsurpassed, offering an unhindered view in all directions.

Middleham
Castle

JERVAULX ABBEY

START Jervaulx   Grid ref. SD 169856

DISTANCE 7¼ miles

ORDNANCE SURVEY MAPS
1:50,000
Landranger 99 - Northallerton & Ripon
1:25,000
Explorer 302 - Northallerton & Thirsk

ACCESS Start from the car park at Jervaulx Abbey on the A6108, alongside the tearooms. Even if visiting the abbey during the walk, please adhere to the request to support the honesty box. Jervaulx is served by Masham-Leyburn buses.

Easy, level walking through parkland and by riverbank. A good, very short option is to walk to Cover Bridge for lunch and then back the same way on a delectable section of riverbank path.

S The tearooms offer morning coffee, lunches and afternoon teas, with crafts and gifts on sale. There are toilets in the car park. **Returning to the road, the visitor's path to the abbey is straight opposite, though officially the public footpath is along the Jervaulx Hall drive to the left, going right over a cattle-grid to intersect the abbey path in the park. The thin path to the abbey runs straight on.** Though perhaps best saved for the end, it is difficult not to go exploring the ruins at once, such is their impact on this opening section.

Jervaulx Abbey is a rare specimen, being one of the few in private hands: admission is usually by honesty box (again). A small guidebook can be purchased, and this provides an interesting read and useful plan. Jervaulx was founded by Cistercian monks in 1156, having originated from Byland Abbey, and briefly set up near Aysgarth a decade earlier. The name is derived from Yore Vale, Yore being the old name for the Ure. At the Dissolution in 1536, Jervaulx suffered particularly badly, and much of the stone was carted off for other buildings locally. The last Abbott, Adam Sedbar, was taken to the Tower of London and executed. The remains are in a condition that would have appealed greatly to the Victorian sense of the Romantick, being less 'uniform' than ruins under official ownership. A stone trough by the gate was a slab on which Abbots were embalmed.

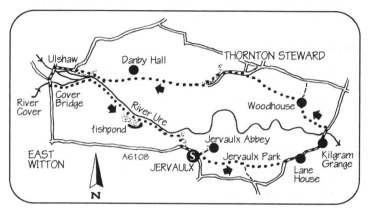

The walk, meanwhile, remains on the broad carriageway winding on through the open pasture of Jervaulx Park. It remains firm throughout, passing an attractive pond then rising to a lodge. Turn left along the quiet road as it descends to Kilgram Bridge. This shapely bridge spans the Ure by four arches and is possibly 500 years old.

Cross it and within a minute take a stile by a water authority gate on the left. Head away on the track to another gate and stile into a field. Head straight across the centre to locate a stile opposite. Some of this section is also aided by white marker posts: the village of Thornton Steward is our objective behind. Normal service is resumed as we head away with a hedge on the right. At the next field end turn up to the right after the stile to approach Woodhouse Farm. Just short of its inner confines go left to a gate, and at the end of this small enclosure, left again. A stile by a gate sends us off to the left, having not disturbed the farmyard. Remain on the hedge-side through several pastures, ignoring the map's advice to divert over the other side for a field-length part-way on.

Ahead are wooded Witton Fell, Braithwaite Moor and Penhill. **At a stile by a small wood, slant up right to find an old stone gap-stile in the hedge then cross a couple of strip enclosures to a ladder-stile onto an enclosed footway. This happy way soon broadens into a drive to rise onto the village green.** At the junction up above is the tiny old school of 1866. **Go left along the green.** Along the way we pass the old pump and the Institute of 1925 opposite the attractive Manse.

At the road end pass through the gate signed Manor Farm and church. As the narrow road winds down to the left, a nice short-cut sees a path signed at the gate into the trees in front. A path through this narrow belt emerges into a field where the path forks. It is possible they will be better mown than your own lawn! **Take the left one slanting down into the trees. In the trees a guidepost sends us the few yards to the right to a stile over the churchyard wall.** St. Oswald's is a very old church, Anglo-Saxon in appearance with a Norman doorway and nave windows. This isolated gem also sports a 13th century font and a bellcote.

A stile cuts a corner to the far end of the car park, where a bridle-gate is found. Head away along the field top, crossing a track and going straight on the field-sides. At a kink a bridle-gate transfers us to the right side of the wall, to resume through more pastures. The parkland of Danby Hall is increasingly evident as lush turf sees us along towards the hall itself. On reaching a bridle-gate and step-stile together, the earlier path from above the church merges.

Advance on towards the hall, using a track for a short while to meet another track coming out of a gate on the right. This is now followed away, through the park along the front of the hall. Danby Hall is a large mansion that was once home of the influential Scrope family. The impressive south front we see dates from the mid 19th century, but the house incorporates the remains of a 15th century pele tower.

The track runs on to the house at Danby Low Mill. Continue along the drive past the house, passing the old mill building itself on the left. The drive runs out in the company of the river Ure to join a road. Go left to the junction at Ulshaw Bridge. On the right here is a lovely little churchyard and Cross, behind which is the Roman Catholic church of St. Simon & St. Jude, dating from 1868. It is a curious arrangement whose small tower is prominent in the locality. The Scrope connection is again evident, with their modern descendants represented in the churchyard.

Go left over the bridge. In one of its refuges stands a curiously sited stone sundial bearing the date 1674. This lovely old bridge of four arches crosses the Ure in grand surrounds: downstream is particularly attractive, just short of its absorption of the Cover. **At the junction stands the *Coverbridge Inn*.** With the walk three parts done, refreshment is surely merited. **Now cross Cover Bridge, the last bridge on this lovely river. Take a small gate on the left and head downstream on a delectable green path. Though we have seen little of the riverbank to date, this final quarter makes amends.**

The Cover's confluence with the Ure is passed in a mix of island greenery known as the Batts, and the path now enjoys a brilliant mile and a half. With good fortune one might see the dazzling flash of a kingfisher on this secluded reach. The broad, grassy strip separating us from the fields is maintained throughout. Across the river Danby Low Mill is seen, then Danby Hall makes an appearance, while later we pass by an attractive fishpond formed from an ox-bow lake.

Ultimately, after lingering as long as possible on these lush banks, the way ends at a gate at the foot of a rough lane. Enjoy a last look back at the winding Ure backed by Penhill high above East Witton church. **Turn up the track onto the road and go left for five minutes to return to Jervaulx.**

Ulshaw Bridge

SOME USEFUL ADDRESSES

Ramblers' Association
2nd Floor, Camelford House, 87-89 Albert Embankment, London SE1 7BR
Tel. 020-7339 8500

Yorkshire Dales National Park Information Services
Colvend, Hebden Road, Grassington, Skipton, N. Yorkshire BD23 5LB
Tel. 01756-752748

National Park Centre, Station Yard, **Hawes** N. Yorkshire DL8 3NT
Tel. 01969-667450

National Park Centre, **Aysgarth Falls** Leyburn, N. Yorkshire DL8 3TH
Tel. 01969-663424

Tourist Information Centre, 4 Central Chambers **Leyburn** DL8 5BB
Tel. 01969-623069

Yorkshire Tourist Board
312 Tadcaster Road, York YO2 2HF Tel. 01904-707961

Yorkshire Dales Society
Otley Civic Centre, Cross Green, Otley, West Yorkshire LS21 1HD
Tel. 01943-607868

Yorkshire Dales Millennium Trust
Beckside Barn, Church Avenue, Clapham, via Lancaster LA2 8EQ
Tel. 015242-51004

Wensleydale Railway
35 High Street, Northallerton, North Yorkshire DL7 8EE
Tel. 01609-779368

Yorkshire Wildlife Trust 10 Toft Green, York YO1 1JT

Traveline Tel. 0870-608 2608

National Rail Enquiry Line Tel. 08457-484950

LOG OF THE WALKS

WALK	DATE	NOTES
1		
2		
3		
4		
5		
6		
7		
8		
9		
10		
11		
12		
13		
14		
15		
16		
17		
18		
19		
20		
21		
22		
23		
24		
25		

INDEX

Principal features: walk number refers